the big book of

HOUSE
PLANTS

emma sibley

the big book of

HOUSE PLANTS

emma sibley

photography by adam laycock

quadrille

CONTENTS

INTRODUCTION

One thing is for certain, the resurgence in the interest in houseplants is not a fad – it's here to stay. There has long been talk of the millennial houseplant obsession, but what has happened to the houseplants that these millennials once bought? Here's hoping they are still thriving! Houseplants are once again part of the social norm and we are living with them as part of our day to day lives. They are just as common in the home as a that statement vase or coffee table book.

We know that surrounding yourself with greenery can help to lift your mood, inspire ideas and create a sense of calm, but did you know that houseplants can also purify the air around you by reducing airborne dust particles and removing pollutants? There is such a variety available these days that you will be spoilt for choice when deciding between the various patterned leaves of a Calathea (see page 110) or whether you prefer the pancake leaf shape of the Pilea (see page 39) or the deeply cut out Mini Monstera (see page 71). In this book we also discover some of the more unusual and hard-to-find plants, such as the Philodendron Pink Princess (see page 36) and the strange little furry Marimo Moss balls (see page 104). We will help you nurture and care for your individual plants, explaining when and how to water, how much or little sun is needed and how to propagate each plant in order to grow or share your collection. So read on for everything you need to know to help you on your houseplant journey!

CHOOSING A PLANT

When selecting a houseplant, I need to know where I am going to put it before I bring it home. It can be quite an addictive activity as you never seem to have enough and there is always room for one more. I like to stick to the rule of only allowing myself to buy a new plant when I know I have cracked the care of all my others, because houseplant overwhelm is real!

But this is how your houseplant collection will start, you will find ones which like to sit next to each other; learn that the ferns and Calathea can be friends because they both like a high humidity so will enjoy a good misting, but keep these away from your Begonia Maculata as it can be fatal if these get too much water on their leaves.

Have a think about where you want your new plant to sit. If it is in a south-facing room with bright sun, then you may want to take a look at the cacti and succulents; or if it is a shelf in the bathroom that needs something trailing, a Pothos may be your best friend.

Another way to start and grow your collection is through organised plant swaps or by trading cuttings with your friends, as the previous owners can tell you what the plant likes and how it thrives. Obviously each home is different in terms of heat, sun and humidity so you will still need to find the right position for you, but gaining insight from a fellow plant parent is one of the best ways to grow and nurture your collection.

POTTING AND TOOLS

Getting to grips with the basics will help you get the most out of your houseplants. Here's how:

- Most plants you bring home will come in plastic black or terracotta pots. These will need to either be placed inside another decorative pot without a hole so that the plastic pots can drain through, or alternatively you can use a dish under the original pot.

- For most houseplants a general potting or multipurpose compost will be sufficient. We always suggest going peat-free as it is incredibly harmful to the environment to take peat and use it for compost.

- It is a good idea to get yourself a small pair of snips – these will be very helpful when pruning and propagating your houseplants. You can also use normal kitchen scissors as long as they are clean and nice and sharp.

- A small watering can and mister are essential for keeping humidity high and your plants hydrated.

- A pebble tray and pebbles for adding humidity to a collection of plants is also ideal to have around (see page 15).

- A moss pole or supply of gardening canes will be perfect for propping up Philodendrons, Begonias and any other trailing plants that you would like to train to grow upwards.

HOUSEPLANT PLACEMENT

Finding the perfect place for your houseplants is crucial, but it may also take some trial and error and that's ok! Testing the position of your houseplants throughout the summer growing months is the easiest way to see if you have them in the optimum positions, as most plants will be looking their best throughout spring/summer, shooting out new leaves and flowering if they are that way inclined. If after feeding and watering your plant still seems to be struggling, it may be time for a change of position. If there doesn't seem to be much growth try moving to a sunnier spot, or if you notice brown and crispy leaves then it may be getting too much sun. As the cooler and darker months set in during winter you may again have to change the position, although many plants do go dormant during winter. Tropical leafy plants such as Fiddle Leaf Fig and Alocasia Elephant Ear will need to be moved to a brighter space to keep them thriving, while you will need to move your Caladium tubers to a dark corner whilst they rest until the spring.

No home or office is the same, so this is just a basic guide that should be able to help you along the way. All houseplants grow at different rates and the position in which you place your plant and how much light and heat it gets will influence its growth, for example the exact same plant may grow far quicker in your bright south facing front room compared to your best friend's

darker hallway, – you just need to work with the spaces that you have. As a general rule, Cacti and Succulents will love a bright windowsill or conservatory – they thrive in dry desert conditions so keep them out of the bathroom as the condensation can cause them to rot. Make room in the bathroom for your leafy jungle friends such as Calathea, Pothos and even a cheese plant if you have the room, or keep these in a room that has bright but filtered sun, placed in a group on a pebble tray to encourage a humid microclimate around the leaves.

It might sound obvious, but remember that plants grow! For example, you brought home a sweet little Monstera, popped it in the corner of your front room, only to find two years later you are having to battle to watch the TV around this now giant! This is when you can really take advantage of a spring repot – try dividing or propagating to split the plant and gift to a friend or bulk out your own collection.

ADDING HUMIDITY TO YOUR COLLECTION

Many houseplants require a high humidity in order to flourish. Unfortunately due to central heating most environments found in the home are very dry and you will need to aid the humidity in the surrounding environment. The bathroom is a great place for plants that require a high humidity as the moisture from the bath and shower will add to the humidity in the air, just make sure your bathroom does have natural light though as this can often be forgotten. There are a few ways that you can aid a humid environment for your plants.

MISTING

As much as you water a plant this will not help with the humidity, so you will need to mist the surrounding air and leaves to increase this. However double check specific plants as some require high humidity but do not like water gathering on their leaves, so another method may be better for them.

PEBBLE TRAY

Grouping plants together on a pebble tray filled with water can be beneficial to plants that do not appreciate water on their leaves. The pebbles ensure that the plants do not take up excess water and get root rot, but as the water evaporates from the tray it increases humidity, causing the tiny water droplets to become trapped between the leaves of the plants.

HUMIDIFIER

You can find really reasonable humidifiers for the home. These can be filed with tap water and set to a timer to release moisture into the air around your plants, and are especially helpful in conservatories and homes that become very dry due to central heating.

PRUNING AND PROPAGATING

Pruning and propagating your houseplants is the best way to grow your collection and keep everything looking as healthy and full as possible.

Throughout the year it is crucial to trim any sad or browning leaves – if left attached copious amounts of the plant's energy will be directed to this area to try to repair them. However as soon as you prune these sad leaves off this energy is distributed to the rest of the plant and you will quickly see new healthy and luscious leaves springing out.

Pruning doesn't need to only be carried out when your plants have sad leaves or are getting unruly. Trimming back leggy stems or wispy leaves in early spring is a great way to encourage new growth and achieve a fuller, bushier, leafier houseplant.

These healthy leaves and stems that have been removed are also perfect to start propagating your plants. There are two main ways of propagating your houseplants; through taking cuttings from stem or offshoot and also by separating at the repotting stage. You can of course grow from seed, but this is a much more lengthy process, so we are going to concentrate on the cutting and separating methods.

CUTTINGS

Many plants, such as the Pilea, Aglaonema and Spider plants, produce pups or offshoots on their own accord; small replica babies of the parent plant will appear as shoots or nestled into the main stem of the parent. These offshoots can be carefully removed – as long as they have already started to root – and placed in a new pot with some potting compost where they will quickly grow to become a parent plant themselves. Both leaf and stem cuttings can also be very successful for propagation. Trim the leaf or stem a few centimetres below the growing point and place in a cup of water. Within a few weeks you should be able to see a new root network growing from the bottom of the stem and this can then be planted. Cacti and succulents will need to be propagated slightly differently once a cutting has been taken; the stem should be placed on a dry surface for a few days for the end to callus over before being placed in sandy free-draining cactus compost to take root.

SEPARATION

Plants that are made up of lots of individual stems or rhizomes, such as the Pickle Plant or Asparagus Fern, can easily be separated when repotting to create multiple plants. Repotting should only be carried out in early spring just before the main growing season; this will give the new plantlets the best chance of a strong growth once separated. Gently take the plant out of the pot and dust off as much compost as possible; this will make it easier to separate the roots without too much damage. A sharp blade can be handy here to separate the plants, but as long as each section carries a healthy amount of roots and leaves they will be happy transferring to their new pots. Dust off as much compost as possible and repot into new pots, water generously making sure there is ample drainage and enjoy your new collection!

REPOTTING

If you're starting out with a young plant you will find that it will need to be actively repotted every year or so as it grows, however as plants reach maturity they will need to be repotted less and less. This is great news because the bigger they get, the heavier and harder this becomes! Your houseplant should let you know when it needs to have a repot, and this could be for one of two reasons; either the plant has used up all of the nutrients in its current compost or its roots are forcing their way out and are asking to go up a pot size (except for Orchids – these actually love being in a small pot with aerial roots bursting out).

If you are dealing with a particularly big plant, such as a giant Fiddle Leaf Fig, and you are worried that the nutrients have been completely sapped from the compost, then you can perform something known as top-dressing. This is when you removed the top 10–13 cm (4–5 in) inches of compost from the pot and replace it with a new enriched houseplant compost. Doing this once a year will provide the plant with fresh nutrients without disturbing or damaging the roots.

However, it is always advisable to repot, even if this is potentially a two person job. First remove the plant from the original pot – if it is in a plastic pot then move your hands around the outside of the pot pushing inwards to loosen up the compost; if there are holes in the bottom then you can tip it gently to one side and poke a gardening cane through the holes to again try and loosen it. Take your time and eventually you will be able to remove the plant from the pot. If the plant is directly in a clay or terracotta pot and you are finding it difficult to remove then try running a knife around the inside edge of the pot and gently tugging at the stem. Once the plant is released use your hands to loosen the compost and free the roots, removing any excess compost from the root ball as this may now contain harmful salts rather than any nutrients. Your new pot should be 2.5–5 cm (1–2 in) larger than your original one; any larger and your plant can go into shock. If your new pot does not have a drainage hole then you can line the bottom with pebbles or chunks of polystyrene to create false drainage, then pop a few centimetres of new houseplant compost in the bottom, gently place the root ball on top and use the new compost to stabilise the stem and compact around the roots.

When repotting certain plants such as Philodendron Pink Princess or an Umbrella Tree this may be a good time to introduce a moss pole or bamboo cane to give additional support to the stem. Some gardening twine will also come in handy here to attach the stem to the pole, but be careful not to attach too tightly as this can damage the stem. Once you have repotted your plant be patient, as it may take a few weeks for the plant to settle in and start actively growing again; just give it a nice big water and keep out of direct sun until the plant has settled.

PETS AND PLANTS

As much as we try some plants are for some reason extremely alluring to certain pets. Huge pots become the perfect spot for dogs to bury their bones and tall woody trunks and moss sticks become climbing frame for inquisitive cats. As well as providing entertainment for your pets, some of our favourite houseplants can be seriously toxic to many pets, and for some reason also present themselves as the perfect snack.

It is not known why cats and dogs decide to eat houseplants. It could be due to a nutrient deficiency that they are trying to remedy or if they are feeling unwell, plants and especially grass are sometimes grazed upon to calm the stomach.

If you have curious pets and are looking for a large statement plant for your home then steer clear of a weeping fig and instead look at Banana plants or Kentia Palms, both of which are completely safe for pets.

Whilst fluffy, shaggy plants such as the Boston or Asparagus Fern may entice a little chew with their playful fronds. They are completely harmless to dogs and cats but maybe keep out of harm's way by raising from the floor.

To dissuade your pet from digging up the soil either place cotton wool balls soaked with clove oil under the top layer of compost, as the smell acts as a repellent, or pop some pine cones on the top to make the compost less accessible.

TROUBLESHOOTING

There are a few classic errors that can be made when looking after houseplants, mainly forgetting to water them or overwatering them! Sometimes your plants will be very happy being left alone for a while, whereas some others need more attention.

Overwatering throughout the winter months, when most plants go into dormancy, is a common error. In most instances you will need to decrease watering to at most once every two weeks as any more than this will mean that the roots may become water logged, which can cause root rot. Other side effects of overwatering are wilting and yellowing leaves and leaves that have started to turn brown and drop off. If you believe you may have overwatered one of your plants the best thing to do is let it completely dry out – most tropical plants may loose a few leaves but should eventually bounce back. Unfortunately Cacti and Succulents are rather less forgiving to overwatering and you may not be able to salvage them – in the case of these desert friends, if in doubt do not water.

Having the compost too damp for your plants can also attract pests. One of the most annoying is the fungus gnat or sciarid fly – these tiny black flies deposit their larvae into the damp compost where the larvae eat the roots of plants and cause an unpleasant environment. The best solution is to let the compost dry out completely between watering as the larvae cannot survive the drought, or alternatively you may need to completely repot the plant. One way to prevent pests making a home in and around your plants is to remove any wilting leaves or dead matter than has accumulated in the pot below the plant, as this provides the perfect environment for mealy bugs and spider mites to thrive.

Too much direct sun will also cause problems with your houseplants – whilst not fatal it will harm a lot of delicate leaves leaving brown marks and crispy edges. If you notice this it is time to change the position of your houseplant. Scorched leaves will very rarely bounce back so I would always advise to prune these back to encourage new growth in other areas of the plant. On the other hand a lack of sun can also have its problems as well – you may notice stunted growth or lack of blooms, and plants such as the peace lily can fail to flower if they are not getting enough light.

Generally speaking keeping your plants free from brown spots, a slight overwatering or direct sun is pretty impossible 100 per cent of the time, but if you take time to watch your houseplants and understand their own specific needs, you can become the ultimate plant parent.

PLANT DIRECTORY

Resembling a sea creature rather than a desert plant, Curly Locks is known for its aquatic sea-green leaves with frilly, pale-pink tips. Unlike many other *Echeverias,* Curly Locks has a very relaxed rosette. Although a very slow-growing plant, after many years it can spread up to 25cm (10in) in diameter and grow to be 30cm (12in) high.

CURLY LOCKS

ECHEVERIA

LIGHT

Enjoying the sun, Curly Locks will be happy sitting on a windowsill with plenty of natural light, but it will also appreciate the occasional shady spot.

WATER

During the summer, make sure to water it well once a week, and be careful not to get water on the leaf pads as this can cause discolouration and kill the leaves. During the winter, water much less frequently; once every few weeks and only enough to prevent the leaves from shrivelling.

FLOWERS

Flowering takes place from mid spring to late summer. If your Curly Locks does flower you will have a collection of bright orange-red blooms.

PROPAGATION

Because this plant is very slow to 'get going', it is much quicker to propagate via a leaf cutting. Set the cutting aside on some dry soil until the end dries out completely, then plant in free-draining, gritty compost.

Native to the southern islands of Japan, the *Fatsia japonica* is suited to hot and humid summers followed by cooler and drier winter months. However, it is susceptible to very cold and dry conditions, so should be kept away from draughts or wind. It has large, deeply-cut leaves that feel as fragile as thin paper, so you can see where this plant gets its name from. The leaves can sometimes grow up to 30cm (1ft) in width and the stems grow out in various directions, so give this plant plenty of room.

PAPER PLANT

FATSIA JAPONICA

LIGHT

Your *Fatsia* will grow best in partial to full shade. Small amounts of sun will be beneficial in the morning and afternoon, but too much will bleach the dark green leaves, turning them yellow.

WATER

Water regularly but do not allow the soil to dry out completely during the summer growing season. Mist regularly to maintain humidity. Hold back from watering as frequently through the winter months and ensure that the roots do not sit in water as this plant is particularly susceptible to root rot.

PRUNING

To ensure a healthy and bushy plant, prune at the start of each growing season in early spring, otherwise they can get quite long and leggy and will not look as attractive.

Native to the dry, rocky regions of South Africa and Madagascar, the Aloe Vera is one of the most popular aloes kept in the home.

ALOE VERA

ALOE VERA

LIGHT

Used to living in a harsh, dry environment under bushes, the Aloe Vera does not need much natural light and is a relatively hardy plant, although it will appreciate a dry, south-facing room.

WATER

Take care when watering, as water on the leaves can cause rotting and watering when the plant is dormant during the winter can cause root rot. Allow the soil to dry out completely between waterings.

POTTING

Use a terracotta pot, as the porous material soaks up any excess moisture from the compost.

WATCH OUT FOR

Be careful if you have a curious cat or dog as this plant is mildly toxic to pets and is known to cause vomiting if ingested.

DID YOU KNOW?

Clear Aloe Vera sap has been used for centuries to treat minor burns and skin irritations, making it the perfect plant to keep on your kitchen windowsill in case of burns.

The Philodendron Pink Princess has grown in popularity in recent years and you can see why; with its pink and emerald green variegated leaves, it truly is a beauty.

PHILODENDRON PINK PRINCESS
PHILODENDRON ERUBESCENS

LIGHT

Pop in a bright room out of any direct sun as the variegated parts of the plant are incredibly delicate and can easily burn. However, the more light the plant gets the greater the intensity of the variegation, so a lack of natural light will cause the pink pigmentation to fade. A grow light can be useful if you do not have enough natural light.

WATER

This hardy plant will thrive in high humidity, however normal household conditions will be perfectly fine. Throughout summer water every seven to ten days when the top few centimetres of compost has dried out. Winter calls for reduced watering, every two to three weeks should suffice, while regular misting year-round is advised to keep the leaves from browning at the edges.

POTTING

The Pink Princess is a trailing Philodendron, so a moss pole or bamboo stick may be needed to provide support for the vine to climb up. Use gardening twine or plant ties to secure the stem.

PROPAGATION

Using a sharp knife, take a cutting at the node of the plant, ideally with 2-3 leaves attached. Wait 24 hours for it to callus over then pop into a cup of water and wait for the new roots to form before replanting in free draining compost. The Pink Princess is mildly toxic to cats and dogs, but only if ingested.

With its enthusiasm for producing delightful, quirky-looking succulent pups, the Chinese Money Plant, also known as the *Pilea*, is everywhere.

CHINESE MONEY PLANT

PILEA PEPEROMIOIDES

LIGHT

The round pancake leaves and its ability to grow in an almost spherical way makes it a great display plant. The Chinese Money Plant likes bright, indirect light and as its leaves and stem will grow towards the light, regularly turn the pot once or twice a week. As the plant grows taller, it may need some extra support to ensure it doesn't get too top heavy.

WATCH OUT FOR

As the stem becomes taller and more woody, some lower leaves may fall off. This may be due to nitrogen deficiency, which affects older leaves first and can be remedied by using a nitrogen-rich plant food.

POTTING

Repotting and splitting out the pups of this plant is easy to do. It will also encourage the growth of the mother plant by giving her roots more room to manoeuvre. Remove the pups when they are about 5cm (2in) tall. Use a sharp, clean knife to cut the plantlets about 5mm (¼in) under the soil, then place in moist potting compost. You can also leave the pups to develop within the parent pot, for a much fuller looking display.

One of the hardiest houseplants out there, the ZZ Plant has been a firm favourite since the 1970s. There is little you can do wrong with the ZZ Plant.

ZZ PLANT
ZAMIOCULCAS ZAMIIFOLIA

LIGHT
It survives well in low light, but equally will thrive in a brighter, sunnier spot (but avoid direct sunlight).

WATER
You will often find the ZZ Plant in garden centres and plant shops looking as though it's about to burst from its plastic pot, thanks to its large underground rhizomes that are used to store water. Many times I have seen the ZZ plant actually breaking open its container! Because the roots are so efficient at storing water, you should allow the compost to dry out between watering. Overwatering can easily cause root rot.

PRUNING
The stems housing the glossy, waxy leaves shoot directly upwards and rarely branch out, so this is a great plant for a smaller space, perfect for squeezing next to a sofa or framing a window. Wear gloves when trimming or pruning your ZZ Plant as broken leaves exude a sap that can cause mild skin irritation.

A tall, columnar cactus that is usually not any wider than its container, the *Euphorbia acrurensis* can reach heights of up to 3m (10ft).

DESERT CANDLE
EUPHORBIA ACRURENSIS

LIGHT

In its native South Africa, the Desert Candle receives maximum sunlight in its arid desert environment; this should be mirrored as much as possible in the home. It may be a good idea to place this cactus near a window, but watch out for burns if it is in direct sunlight.

WATER

When watering, these large plants need their soil to be completely soaked through once a week during the summer. As with most cacti, make sure the soil is completely dry between waterings, and that stagnant water does not collect in the bottom of the pot.

WATCH OUT FOR

Euphorbias typically produce a white, milky sap called latex which can cause skin irritation when touched. This plant is also moderately poisonous to cats and dogs.

QUIRKS

The Desert Candle will grow small, delicate leaves near the top of its stems. These appear to be hanging on by a thread and can be easily knocked off, but it is perfectly normal for them to be shed every year and replaced by new ones.

Known as a leaf succulent because of its apparent lack of a central stem, the Stone Plant is an alien-looking plant with a single pair of fleshy leaves that fuse underground, then slightly separate around a gouge on the surface. The plant is small and button-shaped, with a completely flat surface.

STONE PLANT

LITHOPS OLIVACEA

WATER

The Stone Plant is relatively easy to keep at home and only requires water once a week most of the year, but it needs special care during its yearly shedding. Every year the leaf pair is replaced by a new one while the old one shrivels around it, but for this to happen the soil must be kept completely dry from the end of the flowering season (early winter) until the new leaves have fully developed in early summer. Watering during this time will not prove fatal; however, it will encourage rapid growth by the plant and extra leaves may develop, so the plant loses its two-leaf, pebble-like appearance.

QUIRKS

In their native South Africa, Stone Plants are often mistaken for pinkish-brown stones or pebbles as they grow as clumps on the ground. The plants have a window on the top of each leaf, allowing sunlight to reach the lower area of the leaf underground.

DID YOU KNOW

The Stone Plant is also known as Living Stones.

The arrow-shaped leaves of this *Alocasia* are velvet-like to the touch. This, along with its contrasting, deeply etched white veins and long, arching stems, make it a great addition to any house plant collection.

GREEN VELVET ALOCASIA

ALOCASIA MICHOLITZIANA 'FRYDEK'

LIGHT

The Green Velvet Alocasia should be kept away from direct sunlight as the sun will easily scorch the leaves. If a leaf becomes damaged, ideally prune back the whole stem in order to promote healthier growth.

WATER

Water freely throughout the summer months as this is when it will be in its peak growing period, and water much less frequently during winter when the plant can be very susceptible to root rot. You may need to support the stem at the base of the plant as it grows to prevent the weight of the sturdy leaves causing the main stem to topple. The Green Velvet Alocasia thrives in high humidity, so it is the perfect plant for the bathroom or kitchen.

PROPAGATION

This *Alocasia* can be propagated via division. A newly-purchased plant may have a few stems in each pot; these can be separated out to create more plants or alternatively can be grown all together in one pot to create a much fuller-looking plant.

Caladiums are recognised by their paper thin leaves which are usually highly decorated with hues of pink, white and green like watercolour; who needs flowers when the leaves are this showy!

ANGEL WINGS

CALADIUM

LIGHT

Your *Caladium* will thrive in bright, indirect sunlight – too little and you will notice the coloured leaves starting to fade. It will appreciate some direct morning or evening sun but keep away from strong midday sun that could scorch the leaves.

WATER

Throughout the growing season ensure compost is kept damp but free draining, otherwise its leaves can become crispy and brown at the edges. A high humidity is also ideal (see pages 15–16), however be careful when misting that large amounts of water don't gather on the delicate leaves. Keep away from cold draughts or air conditioning units to prevent leaf damage.

GROWTH

This *Caladium* grows from a tuber. This means it has a six month showy summer season when it flaunts its huge leaves and then drops back into an autumn dormancy when its leaves will drop and will need to be trimmed right back. Don't be fooled into thinking this is the end and throw your plant away. Instead let the compost dry out completely, cut the leaves back to the base of the compost and store in a cool dark space until the following spring. Now repot the tubers into a fresh potting mixture, water generously and place in a bright spot. Wait and you should soon see new shoots and leaves starting to grow. After a few years, the size of the leaves may deteriorate, signalling the end of those tubers. *Caladium* are extremely toxic to animals and humans, so raise these plants out of reach of prying paws and children.

Known for their flat, paddle-shaped stems that build up and branch off each other, the Prickly Pear family is a fun desert cacti to have in the home. They do not necessarily need much space when they are young and are pretty slow-growing, but as mature plants you will have to find a space for them away from any contact as their spines can cause mild irritation if touched or brushed against.

PRICKLY PEAR

OPUNTIA HUMIFASA

LIGHT
As a desert plant, the Prickly Pear craves lots of direct sun – too little will stunt their growth.

WATER
Watering should be kept to a minimum, as the fleshy pads retain enough water to get them through the dormant months.

POTTING
Opuntia are quite sensitive to being rootbound. If you notice that you have not had much growth during the summer seasons, then it may be time to go up a pot size. Do this in the summer. Select a pot with drainage holes and, wearing a pair of gloves to protect you from the spikes, place the root ball in a sandy cacti and succulent compost. Make sure when planted that it is not top heavy as cacti are known to have quite small root balls and can easily topple over as they grow.

When your spider plant grows at speed and produces thousands of pups, what do you do? Make more Spider Plants! This faithful '70s throwback has gained more and more appeal over the past few years. Displaying your Spider Plant from a hanging basket is a good way for it to grow to its full potential. Positioned off the floor, the long, thin foliage can grow draping down without resting on the ground.

SPIDER PLANT
CHLOROPHYTUM COMOSUM 'VITTATUM'

WATER
Spider Plants are prone to developing brown leaf tips. To avoid this, mist regularly and water when the top of the compost has dried out.

POTTING
Owing to their fast-growing nature, Spider Plants can easily become pot bound. You may have to repot around every other year, using a free-draining compost and ensuring plenty of drainage.

PROPAGATION
If the conditions are right, during the summer months tiny white flowers will appear on long arching stems from the centre of the plant. From these develop small new plantlets. To propagate, select a plantlet that has developed a cluster of tiny starter roots (nodes) and using a clean pair of scissors cut it from the stem. Insert the baby spider plant into moist potting compost.

This almost alien-looking fern has leaves, or fronds, that are an unusual shade of blue-green and emerge from a central 'furry' brown creeping rhizome. The fronds of this tropical forest epiphyte grow tall and resemble the shape of a rabbit's foot, which explains why it is also known as Blue Rabbit's Foot Fern.

BLUE STAR FERN

PHLEBODIUM AUREUM

LIGHT

Bright, indirect light is ideal for strong growth, and this fern can be kept outside throughout the summer if the weather permits.

WATER

To encourage a fast and sizeable growth, the Blue Star Fern needs a high humidity, so a position in the bathroom or kitchen will work perfectly. I would also suggest frequent misting to ensure the fronds don't get any browning on the tips.

POTTING

While it won't necessarily grow huge as a houseplant, the Blue Star Fern can be repotted with several plants into one large container to create a luscious sea of blue-green leaves.

PROPAGATION

Propagation is by division and can be done when repotting. Simply separate out the root ball into two parts (or more) and repot the sections into their own pot, ideally using an orchid potting mix.

Its variegated green leaves with bright red veins makes the *Maranta* one of the more attractive houseplants to choose. However, the decoration of the leaves is not the only notable feature. It is also known as the Prayer Plant as its leaves are susceptible to night and day; you will notice the leaves raise at the start of the day and then fold and bow down like hands in prayer at night. A low-growing, creeping plant, it will be happy in a well-drained raised pot or hanging basket, allowing the leaves to flow freely.

HERRINGBONE PLANT

MARANTA LEUCONEURA 'ERYTHRONEURA'

LIGHT

The bright red shades of the Herringbone Plant can fade if they are left in direct sunlight, so place this plant in shady, indirect sunlight during the summer and move to a sunnier spot in the cooler winter months.

WATER

Water your Herringbone Plant once a week and make sure the compost is damp at all times, but do not overwater. Through the winter months you should keep watering to a minimum. Mist regularly to prevent the tips of the leaves going brown and crispy, or even dropping off.

TEMPERATURE

It is important to keep your Herringbone Plant out of any cold draughts. They appreciate an average warmth and any sudden changes can be harmful. Maintain a minimum temperature of 10°C (50°F).

Native to South Africa, *Crassula arborescens* is usually found in the wild as a medium-sized shrub or small tree. Grown in the home, the Silver Dollar Plant – so-called because its leaves can grow to the size of a silver dollar – is just as happy in a small pot with ample sunlight. With blue-green leaves covered in tiny reddish-pink spots, the Silver Dollar Plant is one of the more attractive succulents.

SILVER DOLLAR PLANT

CRASSULA ARBORESCENS

LIGHT

The Silver Dollar Plant will thrive in bright light with some direct sunlight. A bright windowsill is perfect and will encourage flowering. Without sufficient light you may find your plant becomes spindly.

WATER

Known to be drought tolerant, the Silver Dollar Plant can withstand serious bouts of neglect, but to help your plant to look its best, it is advisable to water once a week during the summer months and less frequently during cooler months.

FLOWERS

During the summer, this plant produces a spectacular show of star-shaped flowers, appearing in small, ball-shaped clusters that dry out as small red balls on the ends of the leaves.

It is not hard to decipher why this plant is known as the Crocodile Fern. With its wrinkled and scaled leaves, it's not too much of a stretch of the imagination to see how these resemble the hide of a crocodile. Not necessarily a plant known for its height, the Crocodile Fern shows its majesty in its wide leaf span. Make sure you give this plant plenty of room to spread out – it will look great on a side table or pedestal.

CROCODILE FERN

MICROSORUM MUSIFOLIUM 'CROCODYLLUS'

WATER

Like most ferns, the Crocodile Fern needs regular watering to ensure the leaves stay green and vibrant. Misting weekly will also help to prevent brown edges on the leaves. Be sure the plant has adequate drainage as Crocodile Ferns are prone to root rot.

POTTING

The Crocodile Fern has a very shallow root structure and survives without being repotted often. This fern is actually an epiphytic plant, also known as an air plant, which means in its natural habitat it's designed to grow attached to the trunks of trees high up in the forest canopy. This adaptation means that the fern can take most of what it needs from its surrounding environment, capturing water and nutrients from the air.

TEMPERATURE

To keep the Crocodile Fern happy, don't let it get too cold, sit it away from draughts and ensure that the air is humid.

The Rubber Plant can be difficult to get going from a pup, and the plant needs ample light to avoid leaf drop, but once established there is no stopping this statuesque plant!

RUBBER PLANT

FICUS ELASTICA

WATER

Rubber Plants are thirsty, so water thoroughly once a week throughout the summer, ensuring the compost is soaked through. Make sure there is ample drainage as the roots do not enjoy sitting in water and they are quickly prone to root rot.

GROWTH AND CARE

Regularly wipe the leaves with a damp cloth to keep them looking shiny, and make sure they receive the maximum amount of light each day for a happy and healthy plant. Rotate the plant about once a month to ensure even growth.

PRUNING

Like the Fiddle Leaf Fig (see page 187), it is possible to train the Rubber Plant into a tree-like specimen. Undertake any extensive pruning in spring and early summer to encourage new growth. When pruning a Rubber Plant, watch out for the sticky white sap that seeps from cuts. It is a skin irritant, so wearing gloves is advisable. When the Rubber Plant reaches the desired height, prune the top leaves to prevent any new vertical growth and encourage horizontal leaves to develop, making the plant fuller.

A very decorative jungle cactus, you will find this epiphytic plant hanging from the trees in Bolivia and other areas of South America. At home, this cactus will be happy in a hanging basket or on a shelf that allows its limbs room to grow without cramping.

FOREST CACTUS

LEPISMIUM BOLIVIANUM

LIGHT

As you would expect from a jungle plant, the Forest Cactus will thrive in the shade; however, occasional exposure to sunlight will strengthen the plant and encourage flowering.

WATER

This cactus appreciates being kept damp, so use a mister to spray it once a week. Add a little water to the compost once every two weeks, but do not allow the roots to sit in damp soil, as this can prove fatal.

FLOWERS

Flowering usually occurs throughout the summer months. Bright orange-pink blooms appear along the edges of the stems, and these may last for a few weeks.

PROPAGATION

Relatively easy to propagate from a cutting, you can root the Forest Cactus in a gritty soil mixture in a few short weeks. Make sure that you keep the soil dry until roots have formed, otherwise the cutting may rot.

You will find a Jade Plant, or Money Tree, in many plant-loving homes, whether as a small succulent in a window pot or as a much larger, mature plant that is starting to resemble a miniature tree.

JADE PLANT

CRASSULA OVATA

LIGHT

The Jade Plant is a relatively easy succulent to keep alive. Place it in bright, indirect light for most of the year, but in the cooler winter months a few hours a day of direct sun will be appreciated to stop any leaf dropping.

POTTING

As the Jade Plant matures, you may need to support the heavy stems with some garden canes. Use garden twine to tie the stems loosely to the cane so that the plant can grow tall and strong.

PROPAGATION

Jade Plants are easy to propagate from stem cuttings. Using a clean pair of scissors or snips, cut a piece of stem above a node, at least 5–7.5cm (2–3in) long. Remove any sets of leaves towards the bottom of the stem. Set the cutting on one side for a day or two to form a callous before planting in a soil suitable for succulents. Only water the soil once roots emerge, in about two weeks' time. Once mature, rotate the Jade Plant once a year for equal, round growth.

The *Yucca* is naturally found in South America so can handle most conditions. This woody and dominating houseplant with its spiky, strong leaves make it a sturdy choice and can add structure to any houseplant collection.

YUCCA

YUCCA ELEPHANTIPES

LIGHT

Provide your Yucca with as much light as possible. It can cope with small amounts of direct light during winter as this will encourage strong leaves, but keep it out of direct sun during the warm summer months. Low light can result in droopy or saggy leaves, so if this happens move the plant to a brighter and sunnier spot.

WATER

Water quite liberally from spring to autumn, but make sure your Yucca is planted in free-draining compost as it is susceptible to root rot. Decrease winter watering to a couple of times a month and only water when the compost has completely dried out. Misting is not necessary.

PROPAGATION

The Yucca will often sprout small offsets at the base of its stem, which can be taken out and repotted.

POTTING

Repot your Yucca every two years in spring. It has a tendency to become top heavy so planting it in a deep container will help prevent it from toppling over.

The Philodendron Minima, often referred to as the Mini Monstera due to its similarity to the larger, better-known Swiss Cheese Plant is a small plant that will grow and grow fast! For me, this plant resembles a mixture between the Devil's Ivy (see page 204) and Swiss Cheese Plant (see page 147) – a tall, vine-like plant with the distinctive cut leaves of the Monstera that attaches itself to trees and walls for stability.

MINI MONSTERA

RHAPHIDOPHORA TETRASPERMA

POTTING

The Mini Monstera will continue to grow taller without much need for repotting. A small pot will suffice for the first few years, although the attractive wavy stem will probably need a plant support such as a bamboo cane, gardening cane or small moss stick with some plant clips. Propagate it in the same way as for the Swiss Cheese Plant (see page 147).

GROWTH

The Mini Monstera's focus is on growing upwards rather than outwards, so you will not get the width with this plant. It is also one of those plants that as much as the stem grows taller, the leaves will always seem to stay the same size at around 15–20cm (6–8in).

A fast-growing plant native to South Africa and part of the stacked *Crassula* genus, the leaves of the String of Buttons grow on top of each other, with the stem running directly through the middle of each leaf. Although it seems to grow in separate stems, the String of Buttons is somewhat shrubby, branching off in all directions.

STRING OF BUTTONS

CRASSULA PERFORATA 'VARIEGATA'

LIGHT

The String of Buttons flourishes in indirect sunlight or light shade. Avoid direct sunlight, as this may burn the plant's leaves; however, brighter light will bring out luscious red tones on the leaf tips.

GROWTH

This fast-growing succulent can grow as tall as 46cm (18in) with leaves 2.5cm (1in) long. Although these plants are easy to grow, they are extremely susceptible to mealy bugs and fungal diseases. If you do discover an infestation of mealy bugs then you can make a simple soap spray. Mix 1 litre (4 cups) water with ¼ tsp of washing-up liquid and apply the solution by gently spraying the affected areas. Start by testing a small area to see whether the plant reacts to the solution.

POTTING

Due to its creeping nature, your String of Buttons may need repotting every year or two. Make sure the compost is completely dry and repot in a gritty well draining mix.

Jewel Orchids really are something quite special, look closely at their intricate dark green leaves to see veins of glitter woven through like a 'dreamcatcher'.

JEWEL ORCHID

ANOECTOCHILUS 'DREAMCATCHER' AND ANOECTOCHILUS 'HAYATA'

LIGHT

Jewel Orchids are terrestrial orchids, meaning they grow on the forest floors rather than on trees. You will find them natively in South East Asia, loving a warm climate and a high humidity. They are well adapted to low light conditions, so make sure you keep them out of any direct sun as this can scorch the tips of their leaves.

POTTING

Pot in free draining potting mix, consisting of orchid potting mix, perlite and sphagnum moss, they will however also grow happily in straight sphagnum moss. A partially sealed terrarium or open glass jar is also the perfect environment for Jewel Orchids, as this will protect the leaves from dust and pollution and create a humid microclimate as well as protecting from any draughts. If plants are straight into a pot you will have to regularly mist and ensure the compost or moss is kept damp at all times, and it is also a good idea to place the pot on a tray of pebbles in water to keep the surrounding humidity high.

PROPAGATION

These Orchids are easily propagated through taking cuttings from the main stem – find a node and cut just below it, then place directly into compost or moss. Water at least once a week and after a few weeks the new stem will have rooted. Like most other orchids, Jewel Orchids are non-toxic to humans and animals.

A cactus without a spine, the Bunny Ears is made up of pad-like leaves, which are covered with tiny clusters of spines called glochids, which are thinner than human hairs. However, because they are so fine, they can cause severe skin irritation even if they feel painless to touch. The Bunny Ears is one of the most popular cacti in cultivation because the plants remain small and shrub-like for many years.

BUNNY EARS CACTUS

OPUNTIA MICRODASYS 'ALBATA'

LIGHT

Used to the bright sun of the desert, the Bunny Ears Cactus grows well on a window ledge or in a greenhouse. Do not keep it in direct sunlight for too long, as this may burn the skin.

WATER

During the summer months water your *Opuntia* once a week, allowing the soil to dry out completely between waterings. In winter this cactus is very resilient, preferring cooler temperatures; it can go without water for weeks at a time, so only water it enough to prevent the leaves from shrivelling.

FLOWERS

Flowers are relatively rare. However, if your plant does flower it will produce bright yellowish-orange flowers on the edges of the leaf pads. These will be followed by red fruit.

These strange and fascinating hanging plants are a showstopper at any size. An ornamental cactus, as young plants the flat, zig-zag leaves grow upwards and only with length and maturity will they start to branch down. Fishbone Cacti are best displayed as a hanging plant, either in a sturdy hanging basket or a macramé hanging planter.

FISHBONE CACTUS

EPIPHYLLUM ANGULIGER

WATER

Although part of the cactus family, this plant originates from dense and humid rainforests, so the usual cactus care should be disregarded when it comes to watering. Ensure the compost is kept moist throughout most of the year, and during the winter months let the top compost dry out slightly in between watering. The Fishbone Cactus also enjoys a high humidity, out of direct sunlight, so regular misting will be highly appreciated. A bright spot in the bathroom where it can enjoy the humidity from daily showers or baths is ideal. If you're not sure your plant is getting enough humidity, look out for aerial roots – this can be a sign that the plant is searching for more water.

POTTING

If your Fishbone Cactus is starting to look a little thin and leggy, trim back a stem and in its place two more will grow. This is a good technique to encourage a fuller-looking cactus in the same pot.

We can happily give the Mother-In-Law's Tongue, also known as the Snake Plant, the award for the most low-maintenance of all plants included in this book. With its sturdy, tongue-shaped leaves, this sculptural-looking succulent adds an interesting contrast to most houseplant collections. It is also one of the best plants at purifying the air around you.

MOTHER-IN-LAW'S TONGUE

SANSEVERIA TRIFASCIATA LAURENTII

LIGHT

Although the Mother-In-Law's Tongue will survive well in a shady spot, it will thrive near a south-facing window with plenty of sun. To help it to get the light it needs, try raising the plant on a plant stand, which will also help to give the illusion of a bigger plant. Because these plants are quite slow-growing, a handy tip to create more of an impact is to place a few plants into one pot. This also means you don't need to repot a Mother-In-Law's Tongue often; in fact, it likes to become pot-bound before being given a roomier home.

WATCH OUT FOR

The main problem with the Mother-In-Law's Tongue is that its roots can easily rot. Ensure it has a free-draining compost – mix the soil with a few handfuls of horticultural sand or grit to help – and never let the roots stand in water.

Native to South Africa, the String of Hearts is the ideal plant for your hanging baskets. Although the foliage is sparse, the focus here is on the dainty heart-shaped leaves, which cascade down the wiry stems.

STRING OF HEARTS

CEROPEGIA WOODII

LIGHT

This pretty plant, though needing minimal care, does require lots of light. When positioning the String of Hearts in your home be sure to place it in the sunniest room.

WATER

When in growth, water moderately but allow the compost to dry out completely between waterings. The roots and stems are delicate, so it is common for these plants to be overwatered. Yellowing leaves can be a good indication of root rot or low temperatures.

FLOWERS

This evergreen perennial will possibly flower during the summer months, producing quite nondescript pale-white flowers that will occasionally be followed by cylindrical fruit-bearing seeds.

PROPAGATION

This long-living vine is prone to getting a bit leggy over time and will benefit from a occasional haircut. You can then propagate any cuttings by inserting the cut ends into moist soil.

These miniature aloe-like plants have become increasingly popular due to their attractive zebra stripes and tolerance of neglect. Native to South Africa, they grow as solitary plants or clump together, depending on the type of soil.

ZEBRA CACTUS

HAWORTHIA ATTENUATA

WATER

The Zebra Cactus is very tolerant of underwatering but should be watered about once every two weeks in the summer. However, it is also very susceptible to overwatering, and this can easily promote root rot.

POTTING

Zebra Cacti look great in brightly coloured or striped pots and containers. It is even possible to use different sand mixes on top of the soil to make the most of their distinctive patterns.

FLOWERS

The plants will produce flowers annually, usually just after the longest day of the year. These flowers are not the most exciting blooms, due to the dormant nature of the *Haworthia* throughout the year, but flowering is a great signifier that your plant is doing well.

PROPAGATION

The Zebra Cacti can be propagated in the same way as Aloe plants. Cut off a bit of a leaf and let the wound heal over, allowing the leaf to dry out. Alternatively, this plant produces offshoots that can be removed and replanted.

This unusual *Crassula* resembles a caterpillar or a candy necklace, hence its nickname, Jade Vine Necklace. There is something comical about this trailing succulent – its stems grow up and then spill over the pot only to flick up again to find as much sun a possible.

JADE VINE NECKLACE

CRASSULA MARNIERIANA HOTTENTOT

LIGHT

Native to the deserts of South Africa and Mozambique, the Jade Vine Necklace is used to a lot of sun, and the more sun the plant received, the more vibrant its red hue becomes. Place in a room which has access to a lot of natural light, but out of any direct midday sun; if you notice the space between the leaves growing or the red colour fading then you should move it to a sunnier spot.

WATER

Like most succulents the Jade Vine Necklace stores a lot of water in its dense leaves so water every two to three weeks throughout the summer months when the compost has dried out, and once a month during the dormant winter period. During the winter you may notice small clusters of white star-shaped flowers appearing – they aren't showy but are a welcome addition to this interesting plant.

PROPAGATION

Simply take a cutting from the mother plant and wait for it to callus over before replanting in a free draining cactus and succulent compost.

Neither part of the asparagus family nor an actual fern (it's technically part of the lily family), *Asparagus setaceus* is often found in garden centres, but be aware, this beauty has the ability to climb and wind itself around your home.

ASPARAGUS FERN

ASPARAGUS SETACEUS

LIGHT
The Asparagus Fern will thrive in dappled shade, but can also adapt to grow in brighter conditions.

WATER
It loves a humid environment, and will thank you for placing it in a steamy bathroom. It is easy to keep hydrated, just ensure the plant has a free-draining compost and mist regularly. Browning of the lower leaves is a sign that you may need to increase the humidity around the plant. Even if it gets to the stage of looking brown and dead, if you trim the plant back completely and continue to water and mist, the plant should revive quickly.

WATCH OUT FOR
Despite the fern's soft, light and feathery appearance, as the plant grows in size the stems will start to produce sharp little hooks that they use to latch themselves onto different surfaces or plants. These tiny thorns can be vicious! Wear gardening gloves when pruning an older plant.

PROPAGATION
If content in its environment, the plant may flower and produce small berries. Plant the berries to propagate the fern.

Asian Pitcher Plants are happiest in their native tropical environments of Thailand, Malaysia and the Philippines, but they have also adapted to live happily in your home. Often these plants are encouraged to grow inside terrariums due to the high-humidity environment that they crave; however, sometimes these sealed glass vessels pose more problems than solutions. It would be best to hang your Pitcher Plant so the bulbous pitcher cups do not become constrained in growth, or even just pop it on a shelf so that they can happily dangle off.

PITCHER PLANT

NEPENTHES

LIGHT

Placed in a bright and sunny location, most species of Pitcher Plant will thrive with a few hours of direct sunlight each day. This will help to ensure the strong growth of the pitcher cups. The more sun this plant receives the darker its cups will start to turn, but if it is not receiving enough light you will notice the colour of the leaves and pitchers fading – an indication that its position should be reconsidered.

WATER

Keep the compost moist at all times and do not allow the cups to dry out. This may mean you will have to fill each one to about halfway once every few weeks. Mist regularly throughout the year to keep the humidity high in the surrounding environment.

GROWTH AND CARE

You don't need to hunt down flies or regularly feed your Pitcher Plant as insects will naturally find their way into the cups.

A show-stopper of a houseplant, the Trout Begonia, also known as Spotted or Polka Dot Begonia, has risen in popularity and demand over the past few years thanks to its spectacularly spotted leaves.

TROUT BEGONIA

BEGONIA MACULATA

LIGHT

A location with bright but indirect light near a window, away from any draughts is ideal. The leaves are excellent at following the sun, so to encourage even growth you will need to turn the pot regularly.

WATER

The compost should be kept damp but not soggy and, unlike a lot of leafy houseplants, keep your misters away from this Begonia as water on the leaves can cause scarring and unattractive leaf damage. However, Trout Begonias do like a humid environment, so it's a great idea to stand the pot on a tray of wet pebbles, so that as the water evaporates around the plant, it adds moisture to the air.

POTTING

To encourage better growth, repot young plants every spring, and once mature every other year. Look out for the plant becoming dormant and its leaves starting to lose colour, signs that the plant is rootbound.

The Cast Iron Plant has been wildly popular since the 1970s, partly because of its tolerance to neglect, and also for its potential to outlive most houseplants and grow to a full and impressive leafy structure. The long, spear-like leaves will grow directly upwards, not taking up too much space as a young plant, then begin to widen and fill the pot as the plant matures.

CAST IRON PLANT

ASPIDISTRA ELATIOR

LIGHT

Although happy in most light conditions, you should keep the Cast Iron Plant away from the midday sun as this will burn the tips of the leaves, detracting from their rich green colour. Make sure you regularly wipe the leaves to keep them free from any dust and dirt.

POTTING

Repot young plants yearly in spring, but leave mature specimens in their current pots as long as possible. The Cast Iron Plant hates being disturbed, so repotting once every three years or so is preferable.

PROPAGATION

Ideally propagate by division when you are repotting. To do this, remove the plant from the pot and carefully separate the rhizomes into a clump that has two or three leaves attached. To create a fuller effect in the new planting, add several divisions to the same pot. They will eventually grow together to form a substantial-looking planting.

One of my all-time favourite plants, this relative of the larger *Monstera deliciosa* (see page 147) is often found for sale as a much smaller plant, but one that has the ability to grow and trail with its beautifully intricate vines. As the leaves of the Monkey Mask don't increase in size as the plant matures, staying at around 10–15cm (4–6in) in length, this makes it much easier to train the vines either to climb up a moss stick from a pot or to hang down from a basket or shelf.

MONSTERA MONKEY MASK

MONSTERA ADANSONII

LIGHT

This jungle vine is found in its native habitat hanging from the branches of other trees, so the Monkey Mask is partial to bright, indirect light. However, if it receives too little light, the leaves may start to shrivel and new leaves will not open fully. If this starts to happen, move the pot to a brighter location. Rotate it occasionally to ensure even growth.

WATER

Although quite forgiving of neglect, the Monkey Mask should ideally be watered enough to ensure that the compost does not dry out. If the compost dries out too much, you will notice the vines lose their bounce and the leaves start to droop. The good news is that as soon as you water it again you will start to see it springing back to life. Wipe the leaves with a damp cloth occasionally to remove dust and dirt.

A large barrel cactus with multiple hooked spines, one of which is almost always flattened, the Twisted Barrel originated in the Mexican desert. Usually a solitary plant, it does not often form clumps in its native environment.

TWISTED BARREL CACTUS

FEROCACTUS HERRERAE

WATER

In the desert, the Twisted Barrel is used to having two months of continuous rain followed by drought and plenty of sunlight. During the summer growing period make sure that you water well in free-draining soil, and be sure not to get any water on the body of the cactus as this can cause burning and sometimes scarring if the plant is in direct sunlight. During the winter months keep the plant dry.

FLOWERS

The flowers are always yellow with a red centre and are produced from late summer until early autumn.

PROPAGATION

Seeds are the only way of propagating this cactus; the seeds can also be ground and used to make flour.

DID YOU KNOW

This aggressive looking cactus produces cream/purple blooms, which can attract butterflies and bees if kept outside. It is also known to produce edible fruits.

Native to Belgium but hardy in the English countryside, you will find the *Sempervivum 'passionata'* forming large clumps between rocks and in crevices. Its vibrant rosettes of slender leaves in a multitude of rich red colours make this plant a welcome addition to any succulent collection in the home.

HEN AND CHICKS

SEMPERVIVUM 'PASSIONATA'

LIGHT

Keep it in indirect sunlight and your *Sempervivum* will thrive.

WATER

Water sparingly: once a week during the summer months, then less frequently in the winter.

PROPAGATION

The Hen and Chicks can be easily propagated. Simply remove the plant's offshoots in the spring or early summer and place each individual chick in a pot of soil on its own. You can also propagate this plant from its seeds, which need to be sown in early spring where they will on average take about two to six weeks to germinate.

DID YOU KNOW

The large parent rosette of the *Sempervivum 'passionata'* is known as the hen, while the little offshoots are the chicks, which is where the plant gets its common name from.

This has perhaps one of the more striking leaf patterns you will see – the large heart-shaped pads are a velvet green with almost luminous white detailing. As the plant shoots out a long stem, called a spathe, from its base, you will notice how much energy it seems to take the *Anthurium crystallinum* to push out the bizarre long yellow flower or spadix, which actually seems not worth the effort! As it enjoys a high humidity, it is often suggested that you grow Crystal Anthurium in a greenhouse, but with some careful attention you should be able to achieve a prize specimen in your home as well.

CRYSTAL ANTHURIUM

ANTHURIUM CRYSTALLINUM

LIGHT
Throughout the winter months it is a good idea to give your plant as much light as possible, but keep it out of direct sun in the summer.

WATER
Throughout the year give the compost a little water every few days to ensure that it is kept damp at all times. Due to its need for a high humidity it is important that the leaves are regularly misted. During winter when the air is dry from the central heating you may wish to mist every day.

PROPAGATION
You will be able to split the stems of the plant while repotting. It is best to do this in spring just before peak growing season.

These furry little Marimo Moss Balls are in fact formed from algae, with no central core, just solid algae radiating from the centre. They bob around in the wild and they grow at an alarmingly slow rate of about 2mm (⅛in) every year!

MARIMO MOSS BALLS

AEGAGROPILA LINNAEI

LIGHT

These little balls are found at the bottom of fresh water rivers and lakes in Japan, Iceland and some regions of Scotland, and because of this they need to be kept away from bright light, as this will cause them to quickly turn brown and start to break apart loosing their spherical shape. They also need to be kept cool, so place away from any radiators or direct heat.

WATER

Change the water that your Marimo reside in every two to three weeks. Tap water is sufficient but if possible use filtered or distilled water as tap water will leave lines on the glass as it evaporates and these can be tricky to remove. It is a good idea to rinse your Marimo when you change the water by cradling them in your hand, running under cool water and squeezing them gently like sponges to get the old water out. When you first place them back into water they may float for a few days, due to air bubbles trapped inside – they will drift back to the bottom before long.

GROWTH

In the wild Marimo are rolled along by the current of the water this is how they keep their round shape. At home you can replicate this by gently agitating the glass to move the Marimo, simulating the natural currents they are used to. Without this movement Marimo have been known to start growing flat!

The quiet beauty of this succulent lies in its neatly-paired leaves that form a basal rosette and in its subtle leaf colouring – each rounded, fleshy sage-green leaf is covered in a soft white bloom, the tips often tinged with a contrasting red.

PADDLE PLANT

KALANCHOE THYRSIFLORA

LIGHT

Native to South Africa, this succulent will appreciate as much bright light as possible and is even happy basking in a few hours of direct sun on winter days. Rotate the plant regularly to ensure even growth and colouration.

WATER

Water the plant sparingly and if possible try not to get any water on the leaves as this can cause them to rot. Make sure the compost is free-draining – a mixture of two parts potting compost and one part horticultural sand is ideal – and allow the soil to dry out completely between watering.

POTTING

This is not a plant that will necessarily grow in height, but the pairs of leaves will continue to grow from the base of a parent set. Repot in spring if the Paddle Plant becomes too crowded, but it does like to be housed in a cosy pot, so don't go up too big a pot size.

Growing to heights of up to 2.5m (8ft), this tall, elegant houseplant has finger-like glossy leaflets radiating out like umbrella spokes — it is clear how *Schefflera* came to be named Umbrella Plant. You can find two varieties of Umbrella Plant: one with all green leaves and one with variegated patterns. Both can be left to tower from floor to ceiling or trimmed and tamed to stay small as a coffee table plant.

UMBRELLA PLANT

SCHEFFLERA ARBORICOLA

LIGHT

As it enjoys bright light but not direct sunshine, the more light an Umbrella Plant receives the more growth is seen. If there is not enough light then it may become quite leggy and the distance between stems can increase, making the plant look like it is balding.

WATER

Ample watering will promote a healthy plant, so the compost should be kept moist at all times. This plant, however, can be rather forgiving and if you leave the compost to dry out for a week or two it shouldn't give you too many problems in the long run. In this case it is much better to underwater than overwater, as that can lead to root rot and sometimes even death.

POTTING

This plant is quite tricky to propagate. The best way is to take about 5cm (2in) from the growing tip in spring and place in a growing solution. This may take a few attempts, though.

There are so many different types of *Calathea*, each with their own beautiful and distinctive leaf patterns. The leaf markings are often so painterly that a collection of *Calathea* grouped in a corner can look like a work of art. Although they are all different, most *Calathea* need the same care, and despite the fact that they can be a tricky species to grow, if you persevere you will eventually get a large, full, leafy plant.

JUNGLE VELVET CALATHEA

CALATHEA WARSCEWICZII

WATER

Calathea are tropical jungle plants, so bear this in mind when choosing a location in the home. They love a humid environment and are the perfect plant for a bathroom where they will thrive in the steamy conditions. You can also place the pot on a large tray of wet pebbles, to increase the humidity.

GROWTH AND CARE

Calathea are very adverse to draughts, so keep them away from doorways or open windows as chilly breezes may cause the leaves to wrinkle and curl. Even new leaves can occasionally start to open already brown if they get too cold.

POTTING

Calathea don't need repotting often, once every two years is about right if the roots have filled the pot.

PROPAGATION

They are easily propagated by division.

This creeping perennial can be recognized by its small, pea-sized leaves, which lace its trailing vines like a pearl necklace. Native to the drier parts of south-west Africa, the String of Pearls is found draped over branches and falling to the ground in clusters, but in the home it will be content in a hanging basket.

STRING OF PEARLS

SENECIO ROWLEYANUS

LIGHT

The String of Pearls will grow happily in bright sunlight at room temperature, but do not expose the plant to too much humidity, as this can cause root rot, especially if there is insufficient drainage.

WATER

The plant's ability to store water in its leaves means that it can be thoroughly watered one week, then left unattended for the next few. Allow the soil to dry out completely before watering again.

FLOWERS

The String of Pearls rarely flowers in the home. If yours does you will see pale-white flowers that smell faintly of cinnamon.

PRUNING

You may have to prune your String of Pearls, as the vines can sometimes become tangled and unruly. Trim off any dead pearls and trim back vines that have lost their leaves; this will help your plant become fuller and happier.

With its remarkable painterly leaves, the *Fittonia* is well favoured among the smaller trailing houseplants. They are, however, not the easiest to keep alive in normal home conditions, as they like constant humidity, so they will be at their best housed in a terrarium or bottle garden.

NERVE PLANT

FITTONIA ALBIVENIS

LIGHT

Native to the jungles of Peru, the *Fittonia* is found under the canopy of other plants and is used to having dappled light, so keep your *Fittonia* out of direct sunshine and place in a shady spot. Too much sunlight can bleach the leaves and fade their bright pink veins.

WATER

This plant will appreciate regular watering. Keep the compost damp, and misting is a must. You will know when your *Fittonia* has dried out as it will become limp and floppy. This does not mean the end of the plant though. Miraculously within an hour of watering you will see the stem and leaves begin to stand upright again.

PROPAGATION

Fittonia stems can be easily rooted using rooting solution or simply by placing them in a shallow glass of water. Within a few weeks you will be able to make out tiny new roots forming. Once the roots have grown long and strong repot your plantlet in moist soil.

Native to southern Mexico, the Burro's Tail, adorned with fleshy, blue-green leaves and pink flowers in summer, is a favourite trailing succulent in the home.

BURRO'S TAIL

SEDUM MORGANIANUM

LIGHT

Grown indoors or out, the Burro's Tail will revel in full sunlight – the more exposure the plant has to bright light, the stronger the leaves become and the more enhanced the leaf colour will be. Inside the Burro's Tail is quite a pale plant; however, if you're lucky to see it in its native Mexico, you will notice the greater intensity of the leaf colour.

WATER

This plant is quite susceptible to overwatering, so be cautious during the winter months and water only once every few weeks. For the remainder of the year the Burro's Tail will appreciate moderate watering as long as there is good drainage to allow the soil to dry out.

PROPAGATION

One of the easiest succulents to propagate and possibly the most satisfying plants to watch grow. Gently remove some leaves from the plant, lay them on soil until the ends callus over and then plant in well-draining soil.

WATCH OUT FOR

Please be extra careful when handling the Burro's Tail, as the leaves are incredibly fragile and fall off at the slightest knock.

A relatively simple plant to look after, the Peace Lily is also amazing at purifying the air and is a plant that is often recommended for the bedroom for this reason. The species ranges in size from small varieties that only reach about 38cm (15in) to large, leafy specimens that can grow to 60cm (2ft) or more. When given the right conditions, these elegant plants will produce brilliant white shell-shaped blooms.

PEACE LILY

SPATHIPHYLLUM WALLISII

LIGHT

While Peace Lilies are happy sitting in low light levels, you will be left with a large leafy plant without blooms, but it's the flowers that are the real attraction. In order to flower, Peace Lilies need bright, indirect light, and even then they can be shy to flower.

WATER

Water Peace Lilies so that the soil is moist but not soggy. Allow the top layer of compost to dry out between waterings; ample drainage is very important. However, they are very good at letting you know when they need a top up, as the leaves start to droop and the flower stems arch.

PROPAGATION

Peace Lilies are propagated by division, which means that they are great for potting multiple plants in one pot to create the illusion of a much fuller plant.

These beautiful plants are often seen with their stems braided together. This procedure is carried out when the plants are young and amazingly as the plant grows, the stems continue to grow in this formation of their own accord.

MONEY TREE

PACHIRA AQUATICA

LIGHT

Growing best in bright, indirect sunlight, the Money Tree, also known as Malabar Chestnut, can tolerate a small amount of direct sun, but too much may burn the leaves. Too little light will cause the leaves to yellow. Rotate the plant occasionally so that that it doesn't grow lopsided.

WATER

Water regularly and do not allow the compost to completely dry out. Money Trees are thirsty plants, but do ensure they have plenty of drainage to prevent root rot.

POTTING

If a Money Tree is young and hasn't yet been braided, it is possible to do this at home. Pot three small stems together and ensure that they are flexible enough to plait. Gently move the stems around each other and if you are having difficulty braiding the entire length of the stems in one go, release and tie some twine to keep the stems in place, wait until the plant relaxes some more and try again.

A plant selected for its highly decorative and unusual leaf shape and pattern, the Rattlesnake Plant is native to the jungles of Brazil and will add a touch of the tropics to any home with its bright green topside leaves that contrast beautifully with the rich purple undersides. Just remember that this plant needs a humid environment so try and replicate this as closely as possible.

RATTLESNAKE PLANT

CALATHEA LANCIFOLIA

LIGHT

Keep your Rattlesnake Plant in a shady spot with indirect sunlight, as too much sunshine can discolour the leaves, turning them brown and crispy. This plant does not like rapid changes of temperature and draughts, so try to keep the environment warm without being dry and do not allow the plant to get cold.

WATER

Your Rattlesnake Plant likes a good humid environment. Through the summer months make sure that the compost is kept damp, and mist frequently. During winter, decrease the watering to once every two weeks as the plant will go into dormancy.

POTTING

Repot your Rattlesnake Plant once a year during spring when the plant has outgrown its pot.

PROPAGATION

The Rattlesnake Plant can be divided while repotting. Just separate the stems into as many individual pots as you like.

The Peruvian Old Man Cactus, or Cotton Ball Cactus, is covered in a fluffy white coat that makes it clear why this plant has acquired its funny nicknames. The fluff acts as a sunscreen against the scorching sun of its native desert home. Beneath the fluff lies a layer of sharp spines, so even though this plant looks soft enough to stroke, do not let its woolly coat seduce you!

PERUVIAN OLD MAN CACTUS

ESPOSTOA LANATA

LIGHT

These cacti grow best when they are exposed to bright sun and should be placed near a window. A south-facing window is fine, but don't expose the plant to direct sun all day as this can cause the cottony white fluff to brown and burn.

WATER

As with most cacti, the Old Man Cactus stores much of its water in its succulent stem, so watering throughout the year can be kept to a minimum. It will thank you for a feed of cactus food in early spring, at the start of the growing season.

POTTING

Generally as the Old Man Cactus grows tall, it should also grow in strength, so there should be no need for any plant support. The main thing to remember is to be extremely careful when moving the plant because it can get a little top heavy, and if it is very tall there is the risk of it snapping!

If you are looking for a large statement plant then the Sweetheart Vine could be the one. With its decorative, cut-out, glossy green leaves, it can grow to form a full domed bush suitable for most indoor displays, as long as you have the space!

SWEETHEART VINE

PHILODENDRON XANADU

LIGHT

Your Sweetheart Vine will enjoy partial to bright shade, so keep out of direct sunlight. Warmth is also key in keeping this plant healthy and happy in order to promote strong growth.

WATER

Water thoroughly through the warm summer months, keeping the compost damp at all times and misting regularly. In winter, decrease watering to once every week or two weeks but make sure the soil is just moist. Even in the cleanest homes it is really easy for dust to build up on the large leaves, making it hard for the plant to take in surrounding moisture, so wipe them regularly.

PROPAGATION

Use a stem directly from the base of the plant to propagate your Sweetheart Vine. Cut the stem and place in rooting solution and plant up, making sure the compost is always kept damp.

There are more than 600 different species in the *Agave* genus and the most popular is known as the Century Plant, thought to flower only once every hundred years. With tall, pointy leaves, this Agave will quite often have white speckles on its edges.

CENTURY PLANT

AGAVE AMERICANA

LIGHT

As a desert native, an *Agave* will tolerate drought as well as appreciating a lot of sunlight – so much so that it will flourish if moved outside during the summer months.

WATER

Easy to cultivate, *Agaves* are happy in any compost as long as it is free draining. Water them moderately once a week, allowing the compost to dry out completely between waterings to avoid root rot.

POTTING

Agaves do best in soil with lots of grit. You can add grit through the soil to assist with filtering.

FLOWERS

The *Agave's* rosettes die off after flowering, although this may take many years. They then leave space for a pup to take over.

WATCH OUT FOR

Be aware that some species have sharp, serrated teeth along the edges of the leaves and can be midly toxic to cats and dogs.

Resembling an English shrub rather than a desert cactus, the Crown of Thorns grows fast into a dense, multi-branched plant that can easily get out of hand and resemble a tangled mess.

CROWN OF THORNS
EUPHORBIA MILII

POTTING
Your Crown of Thorns will need repotting every two years in late winter or early spring. Use well-drained soil and transfer to a pot that will accommodate the roots comfortably without squashing them.

FLOWERS
Flowers are small and often bright red or pink in colour. Usually quite nondescript, the Crown of Thorns can look impressive when in full bloom and is a favourite flower houseplant.

WATCH OUT FOR
The sap is relatively poisonous, and can cause skin irritation and burning. This plant can also be toxic to pets so keep it out of reach of dogs and cats.

QUIRKS
Native to Madagascar, this *Euphorbia* keeps its leaves far longer than any other plant in this genus. It eventually sheds them all, leaving only the sharp thorns that line each stem.

DID YOU KNOW
The Crown of Thorns is also known as the Christ Plant.

A strikingly delicate plant with bright green, papery leaves and long, black, elegant stems, the Maidenhair Fern will need lots of attention and humidity throughout the year. Because of these demands the bathroom is always a great location for a Maidenhair, as the humidity from the shower and bath will be a real help.

MAIDENHAIR FERN

ADIANTUM RADDIANUM

LIGHT

Too much light will lead to scorching and not enough light can contribute to poor growth and yellowing of the fronds, so a happy middle balance will keep your Maidenhair thriving. Indirect morning or afternoon sun without any draughts is perfect.

WATER

Be sure to keep the compost damp and the air around the fronds nice and humid throughout the summer months. Misting is vital, but you will also notice that the leaves shed water without actually becoming wet.

PRUNING

If you come across shrivelled and brown leaves, all is not lost. Try cutting your Maidenhair right back and with time you should see some new growth.

WATCH OUT FOR

The Maidenhair Fern's fronds are a good signifier of how your plant is doing. Its tips will turn brown if the air is too dry and your plant is lacking humidity. Pale fronds are a sign of a lack of fertiliser and when scorch marks appear, your plant is being exposed to too much sunlight.

With a tall, thin trunk that branches with age, the *Dracaena marginata* is a favourite among houseplants. It is also known as a false palm because of its top crown of long, thin leaves. This plant is tolerant to neglect, which is why you may regularly see it in the corners of offices and doctors' waiting rooms; but be assured only the best care will ensure that it reaches its full potential growing height of up to 3m (10ft).

FLAMING DRAGON TREE

DRACAENA MARGINATA

LIGHT

A slightly shady spot with regular intervals of indirect sunlight is the perfect environment for your Flaming Dragon Tree. It is relatively hardy so it can tolerate low light, but if it has long periods of low light then it can become leggy and the leaves quite spindly.

WATER

Keep the compost moist at all times and do not allow it to dry out completely, especially during summer, as this can cause the leaves to turn brown and dry. You can decrease watering in winter to once every few weeks and only water once the compost starts to dry out.

DID YOU KNOW

The Flaming Dragon tree is an air-filtering plant and is part of NASA's Clean Air Study. This plant naturally reduces benzene, formaldehyde, xylene and toluene in the air. But keep away from cats and dogs as it can be poisonous to pets.

This sweet little plant has one special feature: as soon as its delicate leaves are touched during the day they rapidly fold up and the stems start to droop, taking about an hour to recover! This will, however, also happen naturally in the evening. An easy plant to look after, the *Mimosa pudica* will produce the most beautiful fluffy pink ball flowers through the summer months.

SENSITIVE PLANT

MIMOSA PUDICA

LIGHT

Although known as the Sensitive Plant due to its responsive leaves, this should not be taken into account when it comes to how much light to give it. Your plant will thrive in bright light and can also take small amounts of direct sunlight.

WATER

The compost should ideally be kept damp through the summer months, without overwatering. During winter keep watering to a minimum and allow the compost to slightly dry out between waterings.

HUMIDITY

The Mimosa enjoys a high humidity so regular misting of the leaves is advised, especially during winter when the central heating can really dry them out.

PRUNING

Prune your *Mimosa* regularly to keep it full and prevent it from becoming leggy.

Euphorbias come in many different forms; the *tirucalli* genus is native to northern Africa, and will sit happily in a pot on your shelf at home. However, in its natural arid habitat this plant can grow into a tree up to 3m (10ft) tall.

PENCIL CACTUS
EUPHORBIA TIRUCALLI

WATER
The Pencil Cactus needs regular watering throughout the summer months; just make sure the compost dries out fully between waterings. As the plant becomes dormant in the winter months you will only need to water once every few weeks.

WATCH OUT FOR
This plant is moderately poisonous to cats and dogs if ingested so be wary if you keep your plant on the floor.

QUIRKS
The stems of these plants are usually smooth and green, only turning grey as the plant starts to age. Look for the vibrant Sticks on Fire or Red Pencil Tree as their stems have attractive bright-red tips that respond to heat, gaining intensity in colour as the temperature rises, then fading as it cools.

DID YOU KNOW
The Pencil Cactus is known as a leafless cactus. Its many pencil-shaped stems have taken over the role of leaves.

What an eye-catcher this cactus is, with its long, hairy stems that look exactly like monkeys' tails hanging down! If you're lucky, it will also produce striking red flowers at the tips of the stems.

MONKEY TAIL CACTUS

CLEISTOCACTUS COLADEMONONIS

GROWTH

The Monkey Tail Cactus has the potential to grow into a really big plant, up to 1m (3ft) tall and 2.5m (8ft) wide, and will happily drape itself over a bookshelf or hang from a basket.

WATCH OUT FOR

Like most cacti, the fine needles are a skin irritant, so keep the plant out of the way of people passing and curious pets. It is sometimes sold under its old Latin name, *Hildewintera colademononis*.

LIGHT

The perfect environment for the Monkey Tail Cactus is in bright light – it can even tolerate a few hours of direct sun – but if the room is too dark the stems will become very thin as they stretch to chase the light. You will also notice the tips of the plant will grow towards the light, so placing it in a rotating hanging pot would be ideal.

WATER

Water sparingly, every two or three weeks throughout the summer and even less during winter when the cactus will move into dormancy.

Native to Florida – hence their Latin name – these cacti are quite rare due to the fact that they only bloom throughout the night. In their natural habitat the flowers appear after the sun has gone down and they only ever last one night.

NIGHT-FLOWERING CACTUS

CEREUS FLORIDA

LIGHT

The Night-flowering Cactus will thrive in plenty of sunlight but also enjoy the odd bit of shade, so do not place in direct sunlight as this may cause scalding of the plant's skin.

WATER

During the summer months, water well once a week but then wait until the soil has completely dried out before watering again. Throughout the winter, when temperatures are much cooler, your cactus may become dormant. In this period water sparingly: as little as every few weeks. The *Cereus florida* will have stored copious amounts of water in its limbs to survive during this time.

POTTING

The Cereus florida performs well in unglazed ceramics and terracotta pots. It is important that this plant has a porous pot as the weight of the pot provides stability.

DID YOU KNOW

The fruits produced after flowerings are edible raw. They are from the same family as the dragon fruit.

With its pencil-shaped, patterned stems its clear to see why this succulent has coined the nickname Pickle Plant. Native to South Africa, the individual stems grow straight upright chasing the sun and they are so light reactive that you will need to rotate the pot regularly to ensure your plant doesn't start to look a bit windswept.

PICKLE PLANT

SENECIO STAPELIIFORMIS

LIGHT

Basking in at least two to three hours of direct sun a day will keep your Pickle Plant's stem sturdy and happy. If it receives too little light then the tips of each leaf can stretch to find a better light source and cause the plant to become spindly.

WATER

Like most of its succulent family, the Pickle Plant stores a lot of water in its swollen stem. Mature plants are very drought tolerant and will only need watering once every few weeks in the summer months and even less in the dormant winter months. Ensure compost is free-draining and sandy as the Pickle Plant is quite susceptible to root rot.

PROPAGATION

Mature Pickle Plants may well start to get a bit floppy towards the end of the stems, and you can use this as an opportunity for propagation. During the spring growing season, take a pair of clean, sharp scissors and prune back towards the firmer half of the stem. Let the floppy top part of the stem callus over for a few days and then plant. Propagation can also be carried out through division. Take out of the pot, separate out the stems and arrange into separate pots to allow space for new growth.

Perhaps the most-loved of the giants, Swiss Cheese Plants are often seen trailing and climbing across Instagram and Pinterest boards, a favourite due to their huge cut-out leaves and notably easy nature.

SWISS CHEESE PLANT

MONSTERA DELICIOSA

GROWTH

As the Cheese Plant grows in size, it will start to shoot out long aerial roots. These long roots at the base of the plant will occasionally stretch outside of the pot; do not cut these, but gently place the tips back in the compost where they can access water and nutrients.

POTTING

When Cheese Plants are young and growing rapidly, they will need repotting every year. However, more mature plants will only need to be repotted every two or three years.

PROPAGATION

These are easy to propagate. Do this either by separating the plant when repotting or by trimming off a stem. To remove a stem, use a clean pair of scissors or gardening snips to cut just below the nearest node, and include any aerial roots if possible. Pop the stem into a cup of water and wait for signs of any small white roots emerging from the brown aerial root. When the white roots are a few centimetres (an inch) long, transfer the new plant to a pot filled with potting compost.

Have you ever seen such a cute plant? Known for its thick, tightly-curled leaves that grow from a bulb under the soil, the Frizzle Sizzle is sure to stand out in any houseplant collection

FRIZZLE SIZZLE

ALBUCA SPIRALIS

LIGHT

The Frizzle Sizzle will be happiest with moderate amounts of full sun; it can tolerate direct sun first thing in the morning and late afternoon, but too much midday sun can cause the tips of the leaves to scorch. However, too little sun and you will notice the leaves start to uncurl in order to chase the light.

WATER

Unlike most houseplants, the growth period of a Frizzle Sizzle is throughout the cooler winter months. During the summer dormancy periods you should allow the compost to dry out fully, only watering every three weeks or so, and refrain from feeding at this time. Throughout the winter growing months you can increase watering to once every seven to ten days.

GROWTH

In early spring to summer you may be lucky enough to witness the Frizzle Sizzle throw up a shoot from the centre of the spirals – this will house half a dozen or so yellow, vanilla fragranced flowers. Once the plant flowers you may notice the tips of the leaves start to brown, but do not worry, as this is normal. If you wish to preserve the condition of the leaves you can trim the spike before it flowers, depending on whether full green leaves or the flowers are more important to you. The Frizzle Sizzle is not susceptible to any pests or disease making it a straight-forward and interesting plant to add to your collection. It is, however, toxic to all pets if ingested.

This plant is known as the Arrowhead or Goose Foot Plant due to its heart-shaped leaves of the younger plant. An unusual feature is the dramatic change in leaf shape as the plant matures. Morphing from a singular point in the leaf on an erect stalk into well-lobed leaves with stems that have a tendency to climb and produce aerial roots, which will cling to moss sticks or supports. This is an attractive foliage plant that will do well if placed in a tall pot when young; it can then be transferred to a hanging pot when the stems start to climb.

ARROWHEAD PLANT

SYNGONIUM PODOPHYLLUM

LIGHT

For variegated types bright but indirect light is ideal. Keep away from any strong sun as this can scorch and damage the delicate leaves. If you have an all-green specimen then a more shaded spot is preferred. You may have to turn the plant occasionally so that all sides get the same amount of light and to prevent an uneven growing pattern.

WATER

Keep the compost moist at all times and do not allow it to dry out as the plant is very susceptible to wilting. Decrease the watering in winter when it goes into dormancy. A humid environment is required so mist the leaves every few days.

GROWTH

This plant is very easy to propagate using the stems that already bear the aerial roots.

You will have to be a devoted plant parent in order for your Boston Fern to reach a large and healthy size, mainly through a dedication to providing the right growing conditions.

BOSTON FERN

NEPHROLEPIS EXALTATA 'BOSTONIENSIS'

POTTING

The perfect location for healthy growth is somewhere cool, with low light and high humidity. The Boston Fern suffers terribly from browning of the fronds if the humidity around it is too low, so this is a great plant to have in the bathroom. To appreciate the beauty of its long, sprawling fronds, place it high up on a shelf or in a hanging basket.

WATER

To ensure that the compost is kept damp, check the soil every other day if possible. There is an ongoing debate about whether you should mist your Boston Fern. Some plant experts argue this may encourage disease that can eventually kill the plant. A better option is to stand the pot on a large tray of wet pebbles, a centimetre or half an inch deep, and as the water evaporates it will increase the amount of moisture around the plant. If the leaves start to brown and crisp up, this is a sign that the compost has dried out too much. Unfortunately the leaves will not bounce back, so the best thing to do is trim them right back to the base of the plant to allow the plant's energy to go into producing fresh and healthy new leaves.

The beauty in these plants is the metallic silver and purple coating that each leaf boasts. Their striking patterns shimmer in the sun and they are grown mainly for the trailing potential of the foliage. The Inch Plant is known to grow at rapid rates, hence its name. It will do very well in a hanging basket and can be trained to grow up or down a moss pole. Because of its fast-growing pace, the Inch Plant does not do too well with age – the longer its legs get the more leaves seem to be lost near the base of the plant. No matter how keen you are to pinch back the vines, this legginess is pretty much unavoidable.

INCH PLANT
TRADESCANTIA ZEBRINA

POTTING

The Inch Plant appreciates bright sunlight, so this is essential and even some direct sun will be beneficial to the growth and strength of its leaves. If it doesn't receive enough light you may notice the colour fading from the leaves as well as bare and spindly growth on the stems.

WATER

From spring to autumn water your Inch Plant liberally, allowing the compost to dry out between watering. Throughout winter ensure watering is decreased to once every few weeks. Misting will be appreciated, but is not necessary.

PROPAGATION

The Inch Plant will root very easily. Take stem cuttings in spring to autumn and place in damp compost without the use of rooting solutions.

The amazing, almost camouflage-like patterns seen on the leaves of the Dumb Cane are most spectacular when seen en masse, and you will quite often see collections of *Dieffenbachia* grouped together in one long or large pot, giving a lush tropical look for smaller spaces. The leaves originate from one central stem, arching outwards to give a luxuriant, full covering.

DUMB CANE

DIEFFENBACHIA AMOENA

LIGHT

The Dumb Cane will grow best and quickest in bright, indirect light – too little light and you will notice the patterns starting to fade and the leaves drooping lightly. As soon as the plant is placed in brighter conditions, the leaves will bounce straight back.

WATER

Watering should be slight, ensuring the top of the compost dries out between waterings. You should also rotate the plant to ensure equal growth of leaves around the central stem.

WATCH OUT FOR

Be aware that the sap of the plant is particularly toxic. The nickname Dumb Cane refers to the fact that if sap is ingested it can cause a painful burning sensation to the mouth and throat, preventing speech. If the sap comes into contact with the skin, it can cause burning and itching. Not a great plant to have around pets or small children.

The origin of this cactus' name is clear. The bulbous, mutant-like form of the *Cereus* could have come straight out of a horror movie. With a tight bunch of twisted limbs and irregular growing patterns, these plants can look completely different from one another.

MONSTROSE CACTUS

CEREUS HILMANNIANUS MONSTROSE

LIGHT

Plenty of sunlight will help you grow a tall strong cactus, but beware of leaving it in direct sunlight; a mixture of sunshine and shade is perfect.

WATER

In the summer water it once a week, allowing the soil to dry out completely between waterings. However, during the winter months it is important that you do not water it at all and make sure that the plant is not placed somewhere with high humidity, such as a bathroom. Take care when watering, as too much water and shade can cause the plant to become swollen and untidy.

POTTING

A very fast-growing cactus, this plant may need repotting every year. It can grow up to 20cm (8in) in height annually.

WATCH OUT FOR

In poorly draining soil this cactus can be prone to root rot. To avoid this buy some gravel or small stones from your local garden centre to place beneath the soil.

Perhaps one of the largest plants to have in your home and certainly not one for a small space, the *Alocasia gageana* is known as Dwarf Elephant's Ear thanks to its show-stopping leaves. These huge, delicate and papery leaves are upwardly ribbed and have an attractive wavy edge – much like an elephant's ear. These can be easily broken and damaged, so be sure to place your giant *Alocasia* where it won't be brushed past as there is nothing worse than hearing the sound of a leaf being torn.

DWARF ELEPHANT'S EAR

ALOCASIA GAGEANA

GROWTH

Rotate the Dwarf Elephant's Ear occasionally to ensure even growth (as it's tricky to move, try using a low, rolling plant stand that you can move around when needed). If you notice any dust on the leaves, use a damp cloth to remove it.

WATER

As a big tropical plant, the Dwarf Elephant's Ear will be thirsty throughout the summer months, so water plentifully, making sure the compost stays moist but not waterlogged at all times. Decrease watering in the winter. It likes a humid environment, so ideally stand the plant container on a tray of wet pebbles, to provide a moist atmosphere.

POTTING

Owing to its size, the Dwarf Elephant's Ear can be a bit of a nightmare to repot and this should be carried out with help. After the plant has been repotted you will need to make sure the stem is stable.

A fast-growing epiphytic plant found growing in the angles of trees and on rock faces in Brazil, the stems of the Bottle Cactus start out pointed and erect but droop under their own weight as they have neither spines or a central stem. A perfect plant to pop in a hanging basket, the Bottle Cactus will also grow tall in a pot with the help of a few supporting sticks.

BOTTLE CACTUS
HATIORA SALICORNIOIDES

LIGHT
This cactus struggles in direct sunlight, but will enjoy a free-draining pot placed in a cool, shady area of the home. Plenty of sunlight is needed for growth and production of flowers, but the Bottle Cactus will be much happier in full shade.

FLOWERS
The tiny bright-orange flowers contrast beautifully with the green of the stems. They then develop into translucent green berries with a reddish tip.

PROPAGATION
Self-propagating, any offshoots will easily root to form a new plant. This may outgrow the original plant in time.

DID YOU KNOW
The name Bottle Cactus comes from the small segments of the stems that seem to resemble tiny upside-down beer bottles. These small, droopy stems are bright green in colour and sometimes speckled with a purple haze. The Bottle Cactus is also known as Dancing Bones and Spice Cactus.

This plant could have come straight from the Jurassic period. With its vibrant green arrow-shaped leaves lined with the faded darker green, it becomes obvious where this plant got the nickname Dragon Scale.

DRAGON SCALE
ALOCASIA 'DRAGON SCALE'

LIGHT

Like most *Alocasia*, this plant enjoys a bright but indirect sunlight, but keep it warm and do not allow it to sit in a cold, dark corner as this will stunt the growth and cause the vibrant colour of the leaves to fade.

WATER

Water regularly in summer, about once a week, but allow the compost to dry out slightly before re-watering. The roots of this plant are particularly susceptible to root rot so do not completely soak the compost or leave the roots in a dish of water. During winter, water less frequently, allowing the compost to almost completely dry out. Mist throughout the year, as it thrives in the humidity.

PRUNING

Remove any yellow or brown leaves, especially if you spot any black spots, as this could be a sign of fungal disease.

WATCH OUT FOR

Alocasia can be poisonous to pets and small children so keep out of their reach.

It is easy to see why the *Euphorbia lactea* is also known as the Coral Cactus. With its erect spine and fan-like, coral-pink oceanic branches, this plant is widely grown as an ornamental houseplant.

CORAL CACTUS
EUPHORBIA LACTEA

LIGHT
Placed in a bright, sunny position, the Coral Cactus will thrive on a windowsill in normal indoor temperatures.

WATER
Although it is not actually a cactus, the Coral Cactus can be treated in much the same way as one; water minimally in winter and once a week in summer.

POTTING
You only need to repot your Coral Cactus every four years. Repot in spring or early summer in a pot 2cm (¾in) larger than the previous one.

WATCH OUT FOR
Be careful when handling the Coral Cactus. It is used medicinally in India, but like most *Euphorbia*, when its spines are broken off, it produces a toxic white mucus, which can cause skin irritation and hallucinations. This plant is also toxic to cats and dogs.

QUIRKS
This species is created by two succulents grafting together: *Euphorbia lactea* being the fan-like crest, which is grafted on to *Euphorbia neriifolia* rootstock.

At first glance the *Cissus discolor* is often mistaken for a *Begonia rex*, however it couldn't be further from the *Begonia* family. The long pointy silver-green leaves with a pinky underside adorn the long, thin burgundy vines that can either be found hanging from a basket or trailing up a moss pole.

GRAPE IVY
CISSUS DISCOLOR

LIGHT

Native to the tropical rainforests of Java, the Grape Ivy is used to sheltering from the sun under a canopy of other plants. Place the Grape Ivy in partial shade, well away from any direct sun as this will quickly damage the leaves. It will thrive outside throughout the summer months, but be sure to bring inside again as the temperatures start to drop, as this plant does not cope well with frost.

WATER

The *Cissus discolor* is used to high humidity and does not like to sit in dry compost, as this will cause the leaves to shrivel and crisp. Water when the top few centimetres of compost feels dry, and ensure the compost is free draining.

FLOWERS

The *Cissus* may flower throughout the summer, however you will have to look closely to witness the cluster of small white or yellow blooms that line the stem at the base of the leaves. Red or black berries follow, which are toxic so keep away from animals and children.

PROPAGATION

Place cuttings in water until roots have formed, but don't leave in water for too long or the cuttings will struggle to take in the compost.

A bright-green cactus with very straight, columnar trunks, for centuries the columns of the Mexican Fence Post have been grown shoulder to shoulder and used as fences to keep cattle on their pastures.

MEXICAN FENCE POST CACTUS

PACHYCEREUS MARGINATUS

LIGHT

Sunny conditions are advisable. This cactus is used to living in very dry conditions so it will enjoy as much sunlight as possible.

WATER

Mexican Fence Posts can be left untouched for years; they are very durable and hardly need any watering at all. To keep them in their best condition, water them once a week during the hotter summer months, but allow the soil to dry out completely before watering again. During the winter they need even less water, so only add some once every few weeks.

POTTING

As these cacti can grow to great heights of 6.1m (20ft) tall, repotting must be done with caution. The plant can become top-heavy, so you may need to repot once every few years to replace the soil and increase the pot size. After repotting, allow the cactus to stand for a few weeks before watering it again so that the roots can establish themselves and the cactus doesn't topple over.

The distinctive feathered and ragged-edged leaves of the Fishtail Palm ensure that as this plant grows in size it will also grow in impact, perfect for filling out a quiet corner in any room.

BURMESE FISHTAIL PALM

CARYOTA MITIS

PROPAGATION

As a member of the palm family, each leaf is produced from a single stem. This is helpful when it comes to propagating as the plant can easily be split and separated into new pots. This is a fast-growing plant, so you will notice the new pots filling up pretty quickly – make sure they have room to grow!

LIGHT

Like most palms, the Fishtail Palm is a sturdy plant that requires very little maintenance. Although it is from the tropics and partial to some bright sun, keep the plant away from the midday sun. The leaves can burn quite easily when exposed to hot sun, leaving a raw brown edge that cannot recover. If browning occurs, cut down any brown leaves so that the plant can put all of its energy into creating healthy new ones.

WATER

Fishtail Palms love high humidity, so stand the pot in a bowl of wet pebbles, a few centimetres (an inch) deep, and as the water evaporates it will increase the humidity around the plant. Keep the compost moist, but not soggy to avoid root rot and ensure that there is ample drainage.

Perhaps one of the most popular supermarket orchids, the Dendrobium Orchid usually has one thick solitary stem, known as a cane, adorning multiple flowers all the way up.

DENDROBIUM ORCHIDS

DENDROBIUM

POTTING

Native to South East Asia, these plants are used to most climates and will grow in any number of conditions. Pot on in very dry orchid potting mixture and add bark chips to loosen and give the roots something to grasp on to.

FLOWERS

Dendrobium Orchids will appreciate a warm and humid environment and the flowers will bloom throughout the summer season and then drop in the autumn. Most of the *Dendrobium* genus will re-flower by themselves after their winter dormancy, be patient with this and do not over-water.

LIGHT

Place in a bright window – the more sun your orchid gets, the more impressive the blooms will be, however if you start to notice yellow leaves then this may be too much direct sun. Not enough sun may cause tiny offshooots called as keikis, pronounced "kay-keys" to sprout from the sides of the cane, so move to a brighter location.

GROWTH

Most will throw out a new cane every growing season. Once these have flowered, trim the cane right back to the base to ensure the mother stem remains healthy. Orchids thrive with cramped roots, and you will only need to repot every few years.

Famed for its beautiful orange flowers, the Bird of Paradise is an eye-catcher in any room.

BIRD OF PARADISE

STRELITZIA REGINAE

POTTING

Bird of Paradise is usually available as quite a big plant to start with and is a fairly slow grower, so you probably won't notice too much growth year on year unless you repot regularly. Repot every two years until the plant is mature, then leave it to get slightly root-bound to encourage flowering.

GROWTH

Once repotted, the Bird of Paradise can go on to produce numerous new leaves throughout the growing season. These fresh leaves are prone to shredding and tearing, so place the plant somewhere that it won't get brushed past.

LIGHT

Typically flowering in late winter to early spring, the Bird of Paradise is shy to bloom in cooler climates, especially for the first year or two. The best position to encourage flowering is bright, indirect light (occasionally direct sunlight). Keep the plant pot bound and regularly feed it. Through the warmer summer months, if you have a garden you can also move the plant outside. Just remember to bring this tender exotic inside before the first frost!

Perhaps one of the most attractive *Echeveria* with its fleshy lilac leaves, the Perle of Nürnberg can offset to form a clump of beautiful purple-blue rosettes that can each grow up to 30cm (12in) in diameter.

PEARL OF NÜRNBERG
ECHEVERIA 'PERLE VON NÜRNBERG'

LIGHT

This adaptable plant prefers high amounts of sunshine but also appreciates a bit of afternoon shade. In the summer months it can be left outdoors as long as the temperatures stay mild.

WATER

During warmer months, water well. Watering from below is the best way to prevent any build-up of water on the concave leaf structures that could lead to rotting or scarring. Do not allow the *Echeveria* to sit in a pot of water for long, as this can cause root rot. Water much more sparingly during the winter, allowing the soil to dry out completely between watering.

FLOWERS

This *Echeveria* is unique in the number of flower stems it produces at one time. Up to six stems may branch out of one rosette, producing coral-orange flowers from late spring to early summer.

The Eastern Prickly Pear Cactus is native to eastern parts of North America. This thorny plant gained its name from the large, oval-shaped, often edible yellow-and-red fruits it produces.

EASTERN PRICKLY PEAR

OPUNTIA VULGARIS

LIGHT

As a desert cactus, the Eastern Prickly Pear should be kept in full sunlight whenever possible. Direct sunlight is highly beneficial to see your plant thrive.

WATER

The Eastern Prickly Pear cactus only needs to be watered once the surface of its soil looks dry. On average during the spring and summer, you need to water your plant once or twice a week. In autumn and winter your plant will require water only once or twice a month.

GROWTH AND CARE

This cactus is easy to grow but needs well-drained, sandy and loamy soil. Try to avoid clay-rich soil that retains moisture.

PROPAGATION

Eastern Prickly Pears can be easily propagated by taking a cutting. If you sever a limb of the cactus and leave it until the cut has dried out, it can be placed on a bed of gritty soil until it starts to root. Do not water until rooting has begun or the cutting may start to rot.

An imposing, almost otherworldly looking plant, the Staghorn Fern can be found in a pot, its antler-like leaves majestically rising from the centre of the plant. Staghorn Ferns are epiphytic, which means in their natural habitat they grow attached to trees and they don't necessarily need to be planted in compost.

COMMON STAGHORN FERN

PLATYCERIUM BIFURCATUM

GROWTH

They have two types of leaves. The first are sterile fronds at the base of the plant whose job is to take up nutrients and water while shielding the roots. Over time, these basal leaves go brown, which is not a sign the plant is dying, but a natural process and they should not be removed. The second type are the distinctive 'antler' fronds, which are spore-bearing fertile fronds that rise from above the roots.

LIGHT

With their delicate and dusty leaves, Staghorn Ferns like bright, indirect light. This 'dust' should be left and not removed as it is there to protect the fronds from excess sun.

WATER

If you have planted your Staghorn Fern in soil, the compost should be kept damp at all times and the leaves regularly misted. To water board-mounted ferns, submerge the board up to the level of the root ball in a basin or bath of water for about 10 minutes once every few weeks to keep it healthy and the leaves standing strong. Feed it occasionally with a fertiliser suitable for orchids.

One of the most common houseplants, the Hairy Stemmed Rhipsalis is known for its long, rope-like stems that grow from the centre. Used to growing epiphytically in its natural environment, this plant will be content hanging from a basket with enough room for its trailing limbs to grow.

HAIRY STEMMED RHIPSALIS
RHIPSALIS PILOCARPA

LIGHT

Rhipsalis pilocarpa thrives in indirect sunlight in the morning with full afternoon shade. However, this plant is quite sensitive to light and exposure to direct sunlight, which can burn the leaves or even stunt its growth.

WATER

Endemic to the rainforests of South America, this jungle cactus needs watering regularly. Over-watering, however, can cause root rot and weaken the plant's stems. Check the soil before watering by pressing your finger on the top of the soil to see if its moist. Only water when the soil is dry.

FLOWERS

The Hairy Stemmed Rhipsalis produces pale pink flowers that bloom in the autumn or early winter, when the plant is mature. These flowers can last for several days.

POTTING

Prefers to grow in a clay pot, as this will allow the soil to breathe and prevent root rot..

With its dense woody stem, the Fiddle Leaf Fig isn't the fastest growing plant, but given the right conditions it should be possible to achieve the height and density that you're after.

FIDDLE LEAF FIG

FICUS LYRATA

GROWTH

Fiddle Leaf Figs are generally found as smaller specimens with leaves growing all the way up the stem, very different to the full Fiddle Leaf Fig Trees so often shown on social media. Training your bushy Fiddle Leaf into a tree is relatively straightforward. You will need a plant that is a few years old or about 1.5m (5ft) tall. You may notice that some of the bottom leaves have started to fall off by themselves. If they haven't, carefully remove leaves from the base to form a clear trunk.

PRUNING

To encourage the top of the trunk to branch out, take a sharp scalpel or knife and cut just above a leaf node at a 45-degree angle. Over time (about two or three months) at least one or two new branches will develop at the node, just below the cut. As the plant grows larger, this branching process will start to happen naturally without any help; however the wider your plant gets, the more chance of it becoming top heavy, so ensure large plants are in stable and use heavy pots to support the weight of the branches. Cut back when required.

Native to the Americas and Mexico, the Fishhook Cactus favours the arid conditions of the desert, so take this into account when potting. Use a deep pot to accommodate all the plant's roots and make sure the soil is gritty and free-draining.

FISHHOOK CACTUS

ANCISTROCACTUS MEGARHIZUS

LIGHT

Because they need a lot of sun, Fishhooks become quite stressed in low light, and this may lead to poor growth and weakening of the spines. Your *Ancistrocactus* will be happy on an airy kitchen windowsill that gets plenty of natural light but also shade every now and again. Alternatively, if you have a greenhouse it will be at home in there.

WATER

During the winter months this cactus will tolerate cooler temperatures; just make sure that watering is kept to a minimum, and allow the soil to dry out fully between waterings.

FLOWERS

If the Fishhook is happy and has the right conditions, it will flower readily from late winter to early spring, producing bright-green to yellow blooms.

GROWTH AND CARE

This desert cactus loves a sandy soil with a little topsoil and compost. Prepared cactus soil mixes also work just fine.

The Common Ivy is a perfect decorative plant for inside or outside. It works in almost every situation, from cascading out of an indoor hanging basket to draping itself over a garden wall. There are many varieties available, including variegated types and forms with interesting leaf shapes, a rewarding family that will add pretty greenery to almost any spot in the home.

COMMON IVY

HEDERA HELIX

LIGHT

Keep Common Ivy out of direct sun as this may cause the leaves to brown and crisp, but too little light and the ivy will become long and leggy.

PRUNING

If the stems start looking quite bare, trim them back to create a fuller-bodied plant that will start to grow new, healthier leaves.

WATER

Common Ivy needs good drainage, and if overwatered is quite prone to root rot. If displaying in a hanging basket, ensure compost is free draining and you can always pop the plant in a plastic pot inside the hanging basket to allow water to drain without going all over the floor.

GROWTH AND CARE

Common Ivy is easy to train to grow around shapes, such as frames in the form of circles or hearts. Simply take trails of ivy and wind them around the frame for instant effect.

Often used as a natural fencing in its native Peruvian habitat, Eve's Pin produces many angular, outward-pointing, pin-like leaves from its shrub-like body.

EVE'S PIN
AUSTROCYLINDROPUNTIA SUBULATA

LIGHT
Eve's Pin will grow in places with plenty of sunlight or in partial shade, and will thrive in an airy kitchen. Be aware, though, that while this plant enjoys some moisture, it needs adequate air circulation and very low humidity.

WATER
Water moderately throughout the summer months once a week, but allow all the water to drain away so the pot dries out fully before the next watering. During winter make sure you only water just enough to prevent the leaves shrivelling.

GROWTH AND CARE
The Eve's Pin is a tree-like cactus and if happy and regularly repotted it can grow up to 4m (13ft) tall, producing light yellow spines that can reach 15cm (6in) long. The plant produces red flowers in the summer, which are followed by red fruits.

PROPAGATION
When propagating, cut the stem at the woody node where two branches meet. Wait for the cutting to crust over, then place in a loose, gritty soil to root.

Given the correct care False Shamrock will grow into a full purple dome. Do not fret when your *Oxalis* dies back during the winter, and definitely do not throw it away, as it will come back in the summer.

FALSE SHAMROCK

OXALIS TRIANGULARIS

FLOWERS

Throughout the summer months you will notice a scattering of trumpet-shaped white flowers covering the plant. Each flower will only last a few days at a time before dying back, making room for the next. To encourage new growth, pull out the dead flowers complete with stems; this will also help to keep the plant looking fresh.

GROWTH AND CARE

Like most bulb-type plants the *Oxalis* will go into dormancy throughout winter, which can be for a period of weeks. Remove the dead leaves and wait for signs of new growth before you start to water again.

POTTING

False Shamrock rarely needs repotting, even when new growth occurs it will continue to come from the central bulb rather than spreading or sprouting around the pot.

PROPAGATION

Propagate by removing the bulb from the compost (best to do this towards the end of the dormant period) and breaking apart the bulb offshoots to repot.

If you are after an easy-to-care for houseplant that ticks the 'pink leaves' and the 'great for air purification' box, then the Aglaonema 'Pink Star' is for you.

AGLAONEMA 'PINK STAR'

Aglaonema

LIGHT

Native to the Indonesian jungle where it grows under the canopy of larger plants, a spot with filtered or dappled sun will be perfect, and the pink leaves will spark joy in a shady corner.

WATER

Water every two weeks in the summer, allowing the top few centimetres (an inch) of compost to completely dry out, the Aglaonema 'Pink Star' will also tolerate neglect and can survive, if you occasionally forget to water it. Throughout the winter months you can decrease watering to once a month, perhaps twice a month if the central heating is fast at drying out the compost. It will also benefit from year round misting or being placed on a pebble tray; if you notice brown crispy leaves then a higher humidity is needed. Brown soft leaves will indicate your plant is being overwatered; first ensure the roots aren't sitting in any excess water, remove any brown leaves and allow the compost to fully dry out for a few weeks.

PROPAGATION

Aglaonema are clump-growing foliage, meaning their leaves will shoot out from one central stem at the base of the plant. You will occasionally notice smaller pups growing from the compost, which can be split and repotted to form new plants.

WATCH OUT FOR

Aglaonema 'Pink Star' is toxic to humans and animals.

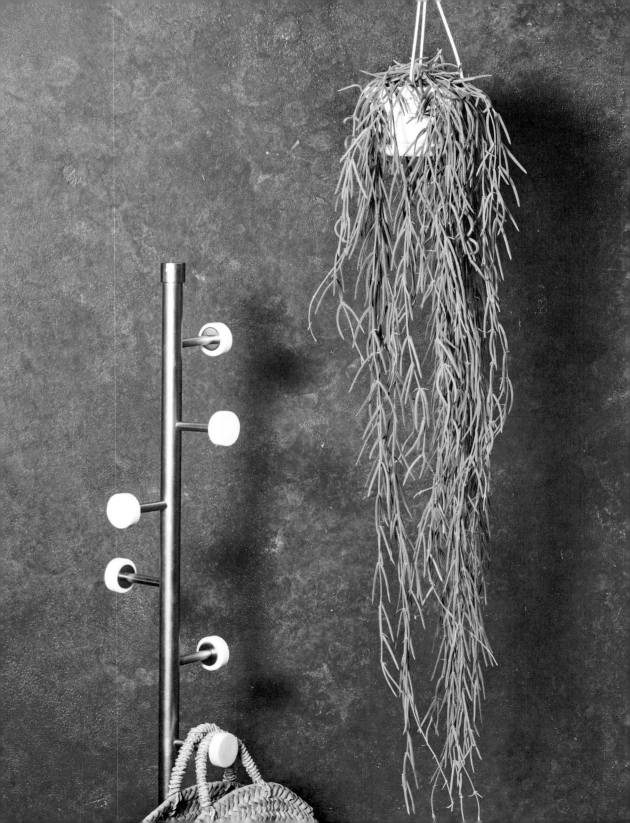

A new plant on the succulent plant scene, the Wax Flower, also known as the Porcelain Flower, is a hanging beauty that resembles rain with its long, thin leaves trailing down the elegant vines. Its common name comes from the small, white, star-like flowers that look as though they're made of wax.

WAX FLOWER

HOYA LINEARIS

POTTING

The Wax Flower is an epiphyte that grows on trees, so as a houseplant give it a free-draining substrate.

LIGHT

This plant is used to tropical humid conditions, so it is perfect for a bathroom. Throughout winter you can place it in direct sun for a few hours as too little sun in the darker months can cause the leaves to drop. Do not allow the compost to dry out between watering.

GROWTH AND CARE

A great plant for a small space, the Wax Flower will grow well, and flower more freely, from a very small pot, where the roots are contained. Each flower should be removed once it has finished blooming. This encourages a new stem to form in its place, ensuring full growth and preventing the plant from becoming bare and leggy.

As a small plant, the Weeping Fig will quickly take on the appearance of a tiny tree. As it grows into a much larger specimen, the very thin, woody stems arch down in a weeping form, housing tiny, elegant green glossy leaves. This plant hates to be moved, so make sure you find it a spot you're both happy with and keep it there.

WEEPING FIG TREE

FICUS BENJAMINA

LIGHT

Bright light is ideal for the Weeping Fig Tree. It will enjoy a spot that gets the morning sun, but avoid exposure to a hot afternoon sun.

PRUNING

You can trim back long and leggy branches to create a fuller-looking tree, but make sure you wear gloves as the cut stems exude a milky sap that's a skin irritant.

WATER

Regular watering and misting is essential to encourage new growth and to stop leaves from falling, but don't worry if you see some leaf fall during the autumn months, as this is normal.

POTTING

If given the right conditions and repotted regularly, the Weeping Fig Tree can grow quite tall, but you will need the space for such a giant! Carry out repotting every two years during spring, and continue until you are happy with the size of your plant. Once you stop repotting, growth will significantly slow down.

This small, shrub-like plant has serrated green-brown oval leaves that increase their red tones in response to drought, the cold or warm sun.

KALANCHOE LONGIFLORA

KALANCHOE LONGIFLORA

LIGHT

Sunlight is important to keep the plant's strength up. Ideally place your *Kalanchoe longiflora* on a window ledge or somewhere with ample direct sunlight. Some light afternoon shade, however, is also welcome, and will increase the chance of flowering.

WATER

When watering, ensure that the soil is left to dry out completely before adding more, as too much water can cause root rot. Water once a week during the summer months, then once every few weeks in the winter.

GROWTH AND CARE

Make sure you pot your plant with plenty of grit or sand in the soil as the *Kalanchoe longiflora* thrives given good air circulation and free drainage around its root system.

FLOWERS

Canary-yellow flowers bloom from tall spikes during the late spring and early summer. Trim off the flowers once they have bloomed.

This trailing vine will drape happily over a hanging basket or cling to a moss stick and climb using its aerial roots for support. With big, beautiful heart-shaped leaves, this foliage plant is also known as the Sweetheart Vine as well as Devil's Ivy, as it is virtually impossible to kill. There is also a variegated form.

DEVIL'S IVY

SCINDAPSUS AUREUS

LIGHT

Unlike most houseplants the variegated Devil's Ivy holds a special trait as its pattern can withstand very low-light conditions, which would usually cause patterns to fade. This hardy plant will still look attractive without too much light. If your plant is all green then low light is also not an issue. The ideal conditions are bright but indirect sunlight. Keep all varieties out of direct sun as this can scorch the leaves.

WATER

Tolerant of sporadic and infrequent watering, the *Scindapsus* will only need watering once a week during summer, decreased to once every couple of weeks in winter. A humid environment will encourage the aerial roots and help prevent the leaves browning, so mist frequently.

PROPAGATION

This plant is very easy to propagate. Just carefully cut one of the stems off the main plant and place it in a cup of water to root. Once rooted, plant the stem in some potting compost and watch it grow!

Just because you don't live in a tropical region where Banana Plants are plentiful doesn't mean you can't grow one happily in your home. Be aware that a Banana Plant can become rather large, so you may want to opt for a dwarf variety as this will be much easier to care for and move around if needed.

BANANA PLANT

MUSA ORIANA

LIGHT

Unlike most houseplants, the Banana Plant will actually tolerate and thrive in some direct light, so keep it in a warm, bright room. However, it will not cope well with cold draughts.

WATER

Indoor Banana Plants actually need more water than those that grow outside, but watch out for overwatering and root rot. Plenty of drainage is a must.

WATCH OUT FOR

Be careful when placing a Banana Plant in your home as the large leaves are paper-thin and can tear and break very easily.

POTTING

Given the right conditions a Banana Plant can grow big very quickly and reward you with a new leaf every week or so. Young pups need frequent repotting due to the speed in which they can grow – this could be up to three times in the first year. As your Banana Plant ages it will happily stay in the same pot for a lot longer without the need for more space.

Despite its tube-like stems that resemble hunting horns, this plant is closely related to the more common Jade Plant (see page 66). This means that the Horn Tree can be cared for in much the same way as the Jade.

HORN TREE

CRASSULA OVATA 'GOLLUM'

LIGHT

This trumpet-like plant grows happily indoors in full sun; however, it will tolerate partial sun as well. Try to give your plant a few hours of natural sunshine every day to keep it happy.

WATER

Throughout the summer water moderately, but make sure that the compost dries out completely before watering again. Do not overwater, especially in winter, when the plant can survive for a few weeks without any water at all.

GROWTH AND CARE

A very fast-growing plant, young Horn Trees may quadruple in size in a year. When the roots start to outgrow the pot it is time to repot. Developing a trunk that grows thick with age, this is an interesting plant to watch mature over time. It can grow up to 80cm (31.5in) high and 30cm (12in) in diameter, and can also be carefully sculpted to create an irregular bonsai plant

POTTING

Propagation can be easily achieved from leaf and stem cuttings. Fallen leaves will also self-sow at the base of the plant, rooting quickly in dry compost.

Calathea are known for their jaw-dropping leaves and the *Calathea musaica* is no different, sporting one of the most intricate leaf patterns, with what looks like thousands of tiny dark green lines drawn onto a lighter green leaf.

NETWORK PLANT

CALATHEA MUSAICA

LIGHT

Originating from Brazil, this is one of the easier *Calatheas* to look after. The *Musaica* will thrive in bright but not direct sunlight, although it will tolerate a greater range of lighting than some other *Calatheas* as the leaves do not easily scorch.

WATER

Favouring a high humidity, the free-draining compost should not be left to dry out. Water every one to two weeks throughout the summer months and cut back to once every three to four weeks in winter. Mist thoroughly throughout the year to keep the leaves looking their best and wipe regularly to remove dust.

POTTING

Calathea Musaica can tolerate being root-bound for a while, so repot every two to three years.

PROPAGATION

Propagate by dividing the rhizome during the growing period. Gently pull into two or three new plants and repot in a free draining potting mixture. Your plant may stop growing for a few weeks after, but fertilise the new pots and you should soon start to see new growth.

This is a complex-looking trailing plant that has long, slender, hair-like runners that can reach up to 1m (3ft) long and house miniature plants on the ends. Ideally, plant it in a hanging pot to give it enough space so that the runners don't get too tangled. Throughout the summer months you may also see some small, insignificant flowers gathering; however, these plants are grown mainly for their olive-green leaf pattern and their strange growing habits rather than their flowers.

MOTHER-OF-THOUSANDS

SAXIFRAGA SARMENTOSA

LIGHT

Keep away from direct sunshine, although the *Saxifraga* will thrive in a brightly lit spot, which will encourage summer flowering.

WATER

During the summer growing period, water your plant freely and do not allow the compost to dry out. In winter, keep watering to a minimum as the *Saxifraga* is especially susceptible to root rot. Occasional misting will also be welcomed.

PROPAGATION

This is a very easy plant to propagate. Take one of the young plantlets and pin it down in a small pot of compost until it roots, then cut off the stem and plant.

Moth Orchids usually sport one long central stem, often curved, that houses many exotic flowers which can last for up to a month if cared for correctly.

MOTH ORCHID
PHALAENOPSIS ORCHID

LIGHT

During the summer months place your Moth Orchid in a bright spot out of any direct sun, as this can scorch the large paddle-shaped leaves. In the cooler months your orchid will appreciate some direct winter sun. The leaves are a perfect indicator on lighting levels; too little light and the leaves will start to turn a dark green, too much and they will fade to a yellow hue. Rotate your plant throughout the year to ensure a nice even growth of leaves and flowers.

WATER

The Moth Orchid is less tolerant to drought than a Dendrobium. During the summer months water every seven to ten days with warm water, letting it run over the substrate as well as any areal roots that are escaping the pot. Throughout the winter months cut this back to every two to three weeks. After watering you may notice the roots turn from silvery white to pale green, it is this green that you are aiming for. The Moth orchid loves a high humidity, and regular misting throughout the year will encourage flowering throughout the seasons.

POTTING

Moth Orchids like to be housed in a small pot and will start to grow areal roots outside of the pot. Repot every two years but only increase the pot by a few centimetres so not to put the orchid into shock.

Native to the Philippines, the *Alocasia* has become more widely available in recent years, and is a welcome addition to any houseplant enthusiast looking for something a bit more unusual to add to their collection. Although many different hybrids can now be found, the most popular is the *Alocasia sanderiana* with its erect stems, dark green glossy leaves and striking pale veins.

KRIS PLANT

ALOCASIA SANDERIANA

LIGHT

Direct summer sun should be avoided as the leaves can easily burn, so keep this plant in a shaded spot and only increase the hours of sunshine in the winter when light is low.

WATER

In its natural habitat the *Alocasia* is found in damp, humid environments, so try to mimic this as best as possible. Throughout the summer do not allow the soil to dry out and mist the leaves frequently.

PROPAGATION

The *Alocasia* is grown from a rhizome, which can be easily split in the spring when repotting to separate into many smaller plants. The top of rhizome should be planted above the soil to ensure active growth.

WATCH OUT FOR

Alocasia are especially toxic so please watch out for pets and small children around these plants.

There are so many beautiful types of *Calathea*, each with their own distinct leaf shape and pattern, but the *Calathea roseopicta* is one of the most popular, due to its tropical-looking leaves with purple undersides. Like most *Calathea*, it is quite a fussy plant that will not respond well if it is too hot, too cold, too dry or too wet; with the right care though it can grow into an attractive bushy plant up to 60cm (2ft) in height. This plant has the ability to close itself up at night, lifting its widespread arms upwards and narrowing its diameter.

ROSE PAINTED CALATHEA

CALATHEA ROSEOPICTA

LIGHT

You will notice very quickly if you are giving your *Calathea* too much sun, as direct sunlight will burn and crisp the edges and make for an unattractive and wilting plant.

WATER

Keep the compost constantly damp but not soaking, and try not to let the compost dry out fully as this can cause leaf browning and dropping. Do not let it stand in a puddle of water as this can cause root rot. Misting and a high humidity is vital, as *Calathea* are very sensitive to low humidity and will quickly drop their leaves or turn brown. Spray with water regularly, and it's best to keep them on a bed of pebbles and water.

PROPAGATION

Calathea can be propagated when repotting by separation. This is a delicate process and you should be careful not to tear or damage the roots.

With its multicoloured, patterned leaves, it is no surprise that the Croton is also known as Joseph's Coat. This plant will undoubtedly stand out against your collection of leafy greens, although it isn't the easiest plant to grow and is known for its fussy nature.

CROTON

CODIAEUM VARIEGATUM

POTTING

The Croton really doesn't like being moved or repotted, so bear this in mind as the plant matures.

LIGHT

Unlike most of the houseplants in this book, the Croton will thoroughly enjoy plenty of bright, direct sun. During the hottest summer months, though, check to make sure that the leaves aren't burning in the heat. However, if it receives too little sun, the bottom leaves may start dropping off. Wipe the leaves with a damp cloth from time to time to keep them dust free.

WATER

Throughout the summer, ensure the compost is kept damp. If it dries out too much, you will quickly notice the leaves start to bow down and become flimsy. Over winter, during the plant's dormant period, allow the top few centimetres (an inch) of soil to dry out before watering. The Croton loves high humidity, so an ideal spot would be a bright bathroom or kitchen. You can also stand the pot on a tray of pebbles, 2.5–4cm (1–1½in) deep, to increase the humidity around the plant.

Although it creeps along the ground in its indigenous South Africa, *Senecio mandraliscae* is perfect for larger pots and hanging baskets in the home. Perhaps the bluest cactus around, the beauty of this plant lies in the colour of its leaves.

BLUE CHALK STICKS

SENECIO MANDRALISCAE

LIGHT

Blue Chalk Sticks is used to partial sunlight, growing in shady patches along the desert floor, so will be happy in indirect sunlight in your home.

WATER

Because it copes very well with drought, the Blue Chalk Sticks will survive many weeks without watering, although if you pot it in well-drained soil and give it a weekly watering you will quickly see the benefits. Be sure to keep it in a well-ventilated room, as too much humidity can cause the plant to rot.

POTTING

With its small bunching stems, this plant will thrive both outdoors and inside. If you do put your plant outside, plant it in a moveable pot so you can bring in before the frost.

PRUNING

The Blue Chalk Sticks can grow up to 46cm (18in) tall and 61cm (24in) wide. You may find that the stems tend to flop over; if this happens prune back each stem to where it feels firm. You can then replant the cuttings in damp, sandy soil where they will take root.

Regularly grown for its furry, velvet-like leaves, the Panda Plant is relatively easy to care for, storing much of its water in its thick, succulent leaves. A light grey-green in colour, the tips of the leaves develop a brown spotting with maturity; their shape can also become quite irregular with time, but they usually start off as ovals. Originally from Madagascar, this pretty plant can grow up to 46cm (18in) tall.

PANDA PLANT

KALANCHOE TOMENTOSA

LIGHT

This plant enjoys plenty of sunlight, so place it in a conservatory or bright living room to encourage strong new growth.

POTTING

Once the Panda Plant is mature and the stems start to grow down below the pot, it is perfect to pot in a hanging basket. As a slow grower the Panda Plant may only need repotting once every few years, then even less when it has hit maturity.

FLOWERS

Although the Panda Plant flowers in the wild, this is very rare in the home. However, the beauty of the leaves alone make it a firm household favourite.

WATCH OUT FOR

Beware if you have any household pets as *Kalanchoe* are toxic to both dogs and cats

A showy plant often sporting an array of waxy red flowers, *Anthurium scherzerianum* has long slender leaves, compared to the heart-shaped leaves of *Anthurium andreanum*. Both are grown for their showy red flowers, but there are a few other differences between the two varieties. The *Anthurium scherzerianum* is much smaller than the *Anthurium andreanum* and has a curly spadix compared to the straight one on the flower of the *Anthurium andreanum*.

FLAMINGO FLOWER
ANTHURIUM SCHERZERIANUM

LIGHT

All *Anthuriums* need protecting from the bright summer sun, as direct sun can cause the leaves to brown. During winter, place your plant in a bright position as the colour can fade from the flowers if it has too little light.

WATER

Keep the compost damp at all times in the summer, watering once every few days and ensuring that it does not dry out. Decrease watering during winter to once every week or two, but humidity should always be kept high, so mist frequently.

PROPAGATION

This plant can be propagated when you are repotting. Simply separate the stems. Carry this out once every two years during spring before the start of the active growing period.

An epiphytic, used to trailing off the trees in the jungles of Southeast Asia, the Aeschynanthus lobbianus can span up to 60cm (2ft) in length and will provide an unusual hanging plant in your home. For best results, pot in a hanging basket to allow the thick, rubbery leaves and delicate flowers hang freely, without being knocked. Quite often you will be able to purchase the Lipstick Plant when it is flowering, but in reality it is quite tricky to get these plants to flower every year. The best thing to do is to cut back the stems once the flowering season is over and this will entice more flowers the following year.

LIPSTICK PLANT

AESCHYNANTHUS LOBBIANUS

LIGHT

During the summer months keep your Lipstick Plant in a bright spot away from any direct sunlight. This can be altered in winter when a few hours of direct sun is beneficial. Bright sun will encourage flowering during spring and summer.

WATER

It is best to use tepid water for your Lipstick Plant. Water thoroughly throughout spring and summer, allowing the compost to dry between waterings. Decrease watering during winter when the plant goes into dormancy. Water just enough so that the leaves do not start to crumple.

HUMIDITY

This plant enjoys a high humidity, so mist the leaves regularly or place near a tray of water and pebbles to increase the humidity around the plant as the water evaporates.

The Creeping Fig is not the first plant to come to mind when one thinks of a *Ficus*. However, these low-creeping variations are great as trailers or climbers and love to make their way up a damp moss stick. Their stems also like to shoot out aerial roots, which help to cling to such objects or the inside of a terrarium if planted in a bottle garden.

CREEPING FIG

FICUS PUMILA

LIGHT

Your *Ficus pumila* is used to creeping along the ground, so it will appreciate a well-shaded spot in your home. A common problem with this plant is brown, crispy leaves, which can easily happen if it is given too much exposure to the sun.

WATER

Water regularly, especially through the summer months as your trailing *Ficus* should never be allowed to dry out. Frequent misting is also essential to keep the plant looking happy. During winter you can decrease watering but carry on with misting.

HUMIDITY

As your plant grows it can start looking a little wild, so prune it back every spring to rejuvenate and keep it in good shape. The *Ficus* doesn't mind being root-bound to some degree. However, it does like to spread out it roots, so when you do repot your plant, cut back any roots which are outside the main root section. You don't need to do this if you are increasing the pot size.

Originating from Japan and known for its abundance of lush foliage, the *Hosta* has usually been seen as an outdoors plant, but more recently we are seeing it pop up a lot more in the home. The appeal is largely in its decorative leaf patterns rather than in an elaborate flower. They are relatively easy to care for, and if you have enough space in your home, you can let them reach their full potential of up to 1.6m (5ft) in diameter. All *Hostas* have a dormant period in the winter so they are best grown as annuals: do not be too dismayed if they die back after a flourishing summer.

PLANTAIN LILY

HOSTA

LIGHT

All *Hostas* grow well in shade, but this can vary between each variety. Some prefer full shade while others will thrive in partial shade, so make sure to look this up when you buy your plant.

WATER

When grown inside in a container, your *Hosta* will require plenty of watering. Their compost should be kept damp at all times, and make sure they are especially well watered on hot days during the summer. It is important to make sure there is ample drainage though as soggy roots will cause root rot.

REPOTTING

Divide when repotting. Ensure each part of the plant has some roots and shake off any excess compost and repot. This should only be carried out in late spring to early summer.

The appeal of the Sago Palm is its beautiful feathery foliage that fans out from the trunk to form a strong architectural crown. The Sago Palm is not in fact a palm at all, but a member of the *Cycad* family, an ancient group of forest plants that date back to prehistoric times.

SAGO PALM

CYCAS REVOLUTA

LIGHT

Cycads are shade-loving jungle plants that are found on the forest floor. However, they do appreciate a certain amount of direct sun, especially throughout the cooler winter months.

WATER

The compost should be kept damp, but ensure it is free-draining and do not let water gather around the crown of the plant as this can cause rotting. Humidity is also key. Place your Sago Palm on a tray of wet pebbles. If the air around the plant is too dry, the leaves will start to brown. Rotate the plant to ensure equal growth.

POTTING

One thing you will have to offer a mature Sago Palm, is space. Their strong rosette of spiky leaves means it isn't the most practical plant to have in a small space. Conversely, you need to be careful not to knock or bend the leaves as it will take a long time for a replacement to grow. Plant in a sturdy pot and try placing on a side table or plant stand to appreciate the full show of leaves. This is one plant to avoid if you have small children or pets as the leaves are highly poisonous if ingested.

Native to the desert hillsides of the Canary Islands, the Tree Houseleek's woody stems branch out in all directions, allowing their green or red rosettes to catch as much sun as possible.

TREE HOUSELEEK

AEONIUM ARBOREUM

LIGHT

In the home be sure to give your *Aeonium* as much sun as possible to help it keep its circular shape. This will prevent the leaves curling up.

WATER

Care should be taken with Tree Houseleeks to prevent overwatering. During the summer months they should be watered and then left until the soil is lightly damp; however, during the winter months leave the compost until it is fully dry before watering again.

POTTING

These plants are very fast growing and may need repotting once a year. They can grow to 1.5m (5ft) tall so to secure your plant as it grows, pot it in a sandy soil mix.

FLOWERS

You may see small, star-like yellow flowers blooming from the centre of the rosettes from late winter to early spring. Be aware, though, that after flowering the rosette will die off.

QUIRKS

Because of the speed of growth and weight of the rosettes, occasionally some of the branches may snap off. However, these can be used later for propagation.

Native to the Cape of South Africa, this *Gasteria* is made up of two fans of tongue-shaped dark-green leaves. The name *Verrucosa* means rough and warty, and describes the texture of the leaves.

OX TONGUE
GASTERIA VERRUCOSA

LIGHT
Enjoying large amounts of sunlight, this succulent will do very well in a bright and airy room, and will be even happier on a windowsill, although do make sure that it isn't exposed to direct sunlight all day as this will burn the leaves. The sunlight will encourage the blooming of the orange and red flowers that can appear throughout the late summer and early autumn.

WATER
Tolerant of neglect, the Ox Tongue can go for long periods without water, although it will appreciate a weekly sprinkling, especially in the summer months. During winter you can leave many weeks between waterings. Ensure that the plant is in a free-draining, gritty soil.

PROPAGATION
Left alone, the Ox Tongue will form large clusters, sprouting pups from the base of the original plant. These can be left to grow or used to easily propagate a new plant.

DID YOU KNOW
The Ox Tongue is also known as the Tongue Aloe and Warted Aloe.

Native to South Africa, this small succulent is known for its tightly-packed leaves that all grow around a thin stem, forming a square mass. Many of these stems grow together in a bushy formation up to 20cm (8in) in length, so this is a perfect houseplant for a hanging basket where its limbs can hang and grow freely.

WATCH CHAIN
CRASSULA LYCOPODIOIDES

LIGHT
Favouring a room with bright sunlight and perhaps even some early morning direct sun, the Watch Chain will thrive in the heat, as long as the humidity is low.

WATER
Water abundantly in summer soaking the soil, but be sure to remove any water from the tray and allow the pot to dry out completely before watering again. During the winter months, if the plant is in a cool place, do not water or feed at all; resume when the plant is in a warmer temperature.

FLOWERS
A cool winter location can also encourage a bloom in the spring. You will notice small yellow flowers growing from the stems of the plant, and these can sometimes smell quite pungent and unpleasant, so be aware!

PROPAGATION
The Watch Chain is generally started by offshoots or leaf cuttings, making them incredibly easy to propagate from a single leaf. Leave your cuttings to sprout, then plant in a succulent or cactus soil mix.

A native of the bush regions of Kenya, the woody leaves of the Walking Sansevieria fan out to produce a plaited pattern along the central stem of the plant.

WALKING SANSEVIERIA

SANSEVIERIA PINGUICULA

LIGHT

Most Sansevierias will survive in a wide range of light conditions, but the *pinguicula* will thrive in bright direct sunlight as well as a shady corner, as long as it receives a few hours of indirect sunlight every day.

WATER

When watering, ensure that the compost is allowed to dry out completely before watering again; the Walking Sansevieria is highly susceptible to root rot, so use a porous and gritty soil mix. When the plant is sufficiently watered you will notice that the undersides of the leaves are long and smooth. However, in drier conditions you will start to notice long ridges developing on the underside as the plant draws on all its water supplies. During the summer months water once a week; during colder winter months decrease watering to once every few weeks.

FLOWERS

The Walking Sansevieria produces flowers that are whitish to pale yellow-green; however, they are not known for their ornamental qualities.

With its paper-thin leaves that boast the most bright and beautiful pink, green and white details, this is a small showstopper of a houseplant. Originating from Madagascar, the Polka Dot Plant is easy to grow and look after, but it has one drawback and that is its relatively short lifespan. After flowering the plant will either move into dormancy or even completely die back. The flowers are a light lavender and grow from a long offshoot. To prolong the life of your plant, pinch back the flowers, as these plants are mainly grown for their foliage.

POLKA DOT PLANT

HYPOESTES PHYLLOSTACHYA

LIGHT

Bright light is best for this plant. The more light your *Hypoestes* receives, the more deep and vibrant its leaf pattern will become. If you start to see solid green patches appearing on the leaves, move the plant to a sunnier position.

WATER

Keep the soil damp throughout the summer months and mist frequently to keep the humidity high. During winter, water much less frequently and after flowering refrain from giving too much water. If the plant slips into dormancy, continue to water as usual as soon as new growth starts to occur.

POTTING

Repot your plant in the spring or when it has outgrown its pot. If you notice your Polka Dot stops growing then it's probably because it has become root-bound; so repot.

You will find the Beehive Cactus residing in the desert scrub of its native Mexico or in the conifer forests of Canada, high up in the mountains. This solitary cactus may sometimes clump to form beds of small bodies, each covered in a web of aggressive looking star-shaped spines.

BEEHIVE CACTUS

ESCOBARIA VIVIPARA

LIGHT

Ensuring that this cactus is exposed to full sun in the morning to light shade throughout the day will promote strong growth and increase the chance of blooming. The Beehive produces vivid fuchsia-coloured flowers during spring to late summer.

WATER

The Beehive originates from an area with summer rainfall, so water it moderately once a week throughout the warmer months ensuring that the compost dries out completely between waterings to prevent root rot. Through the cooler winter months reduce watering to once every two to three weeks.

PROPAGATION

Propagation can be achieved through cuttings. You can take off the head of the Beehive and leave it to callus over until dry, then replant it in a gritty, sandy compost to root.

The original Rex Begonia originated from India, but unfortunately this species no longer exists; what we see now in shops are the brightly coloured hybrids that have developed from the original. Rex Begonias rarely flower, and if they do the flowers should be removed, as this will allow the plant to focus all of its energy on the development of the attractive curling leaves. The leaves will often look lopsided due to the way they uncurl as they grow from the hairy stems, but the real beauty is in the array of colours, patterns and occasional metallic silver sheen that can be seen on them.

REX BEGONIA

BEGONIA REX

LIGHT

The leaves of a *Begonia rex* like to grow to face the sun so you will need to turn the pot occasionally to ensure you have healthy growth on every side of the plant. Place in a bright spot away from any direct sunlight. During winter ensure that your *Begonia rex* receives a few hours of morning and evening light if possible.

WATER

Keep the compost moist at all times, allowing the top layer to dry out slightly between waterings throughout the summer months. In winter, water more sparingly. A humid atmosphere for your *Begonia rex* will be appreciated, so mist the surrounding air, but make sure not to get any water on the leaves.

POTTING

You should repot your plant every spring as *Begonias* can increase in size very quickly and become root-bound. If this happens the leaves are likely to lose their vibrant colours.

GLOSSARY

Aerial root: A root that grows out from the stem above ground level.

Air purifier: A plant that can absorb harmful toxins from the air.

Arid: An arid land or climate has little rain or moisture and is often too barren to support vegetation.

Bonsai: The art of dwarfing trees by careful root and stem pruning.

Callous: This is a process that occurs after a cutting is made and the wound is left to dry so the damaged tissues seal over, reducing the chance of a fungal attack.

Crozier: The curled top of a young fern.

Epiphytic: An organism that grows on the surface of a plant.

Frond: A leaf of a fern or palm.

Germination: This is a process when a seed, in the right conditions, sprouts and develops into a new plant.

Hardy: A plant that can withstand adverse growing conditions, tolerating cold, heat, drought, flooding or draughts.

Humidity: A measure of the amount of water vapour in the air. Plants that originated from a jungle environment like to live in a humid atmosphere.

Leaf node: A small swelling that occurs on a plant stem from which one or more leaves emerge.

Leggy: A plant that has long, spindly, often leafless stems.

Offset: A young plantlet that appears on a mature plant. These can usually be carefully detached and used for propagation.

Plantlets: Young or small plants that grow off of a parent plant, which can be propagated.

Propagation: To breed specimens of a plant by natural processes from the parent stock.

Pup: A plant that develops as an offset from a parent plant.

Raceme: This is a flower cluster attached to a central axis with separate flowers attached by short stalks at equal distances along the stem.

Rhizome: This is when a horizontal plant stem, usually situated underground, produces the shoot and root systems of a new plant. Rhizome is also called creeping rootstalk.

Root-bound: The roots of a plant that has outgrown its pot and will grow in circles, becoming cramped and tangled.

Spathe: A large bract, enclosing the flower cluster of certain plants, especially the spadix of arums and palms.

Spindly: A tall and thin plant. This can be unattractive and can weaken the plant. Solve the problem by pruning the spindly end.

Substrate: The base on which an organism lives, soil is the substrate of most plants.

Variegated leaves: A rare leaf which has both green and nongreen parts.

INDEX

SUPPLIERS

Whether you are shopping for plants or equipment you'll find everything you need from the shops listed here – these are just some of my favourites.

CONSERVATORY ARCHIVES

A London mecca for all plant collectors.

www.conservatoryarchives.co.uk

FOREST

Plant and products that bring nature into your home.

www.forest.london

GRAEN STUDIOS

Design-led products for horticulture.

www.graenstudios.com

GREEN ROOMS MARKET

Organises markets and pop-up events for independent sellers of plants.

www.greenroomsmarket.com

LAZY GLAZE – HARRIET LEVY-COOPER

Functional ceramics for everyday life.

www.lazyglaze.co.uk

LONDON TERRARIUMS

A curated selection of beautifully designed plants and accessories.

www.londonterrariums.com

LOUISE MADZIA

A chic collection of quirky planters.

www.louisemadzia.com

POT PARTY

A fun collection of delightful planters.

www.potparty.co.uk

STUDIO NO.16

3D printed plant pots made in South London
www.etsy.com/uk/shop/StudioNo16

THE CHELSEA PHYSIC GARDEN

London's oldest botanical garden with café and gift shop.

www.chelseaphysicgarden.co.uk

ABOUT THE AUTHOR

Emma Sibley has had a keen interest in horticulture from a young age and after studying Surface Design at university, she changed career direction to work with plants. She took a number of short courses to increase her knowledge and love of all things green. Emma now runs a growing start-up business called London Terrariums and offers workshops, interior displays and private commissions. Emma is a member of the British Cactus and Succulent Society. She is also the author of *The Little Book of House Plants*, *The Little Book of Cacti* and *Little Book, Big Plants* by Quadrille.

Managing Director Sarah Lavelle
Senior Commissioning Editor
Harriet Butt
Assistant Editor Oreolu Grillo
Designer Alicia House
Photographer Adam Laycock
Props Stylist Holly Bruce
Dog Model Walnut Wiggins
Head of Production Stephen Lang
Senior Production Controller
Sabeena Atchia

Published in 2023 by
Quadrille Publishing Limited

Quadrille
52–54 Southwark Street
London SE1 1UN
quadrille.com

Cataloguing in Publication Data:
a catalogue record for this book
is available from the British Library.

Text © Emma Sibley 2023
Design, layout, illustrations and
photography © Quadrille 2023

Reprinted in 2024
10 9 8 7 6 5 4 3 2

ISBN 978 1 78713 942 8

Printed in China